OFF-THE-GRID BABY NAMES

the **nameberry** guide

OFF-THE-GRID BABY NAMES

1000s of Names Never in the Top 1000

Pamela Redmond Satran & Linda Rosenkrantz

The Nameberry Guide of Off-the-Grid Baby Names: 1000s of Names Never in the Top 1000

© 2012 by Pamela Redmond Satran & Linda Rosenkrantz

nameberry.com

INTRODUCTION

You want an unusual name for your baby.

But not unusual in the same way everyone else is being unusual. No quirky hipster favorites like Iris or Ike for you, no newly-minted names that are a lot trendier than many people guess.

What you want is an *unusual* unusual name, a name that's truly off the grid, a name that not only transcends popularity now but that's *always* transcended popularity.

That's what we've collected for you here: Thousands of names that have never been in the U.S. Top 1000, not once since the government began tracking name statistics in 1880. Names that are given, at most, to a couple hundred children in the U.S. each year, down to names that are literally unique.

After writing ten books on names over 25 years, we're creating a new kind of name book, one that our website Nameberry makes uniquely possible for us. With the help of our engineer Hugh Hunter, we were able to parse over 130 years' worth of government baby name data against our own 50,000 name database and extract those 6,000 names usable enough to include on Nameberry but not so popular as to ever make the Top 1000.

Then we picked our favorites from the lot — the several hundred best choices for girls and boys (and sometimes either) — included here with origins, definitions, and our trademark commentary.

Included in this group are fascinating historic names that have been overlooked for decades — or even centuries. Also here are appealing international twists on familiar English names, and words you've never considered as names before.

Unusual names can be memorable and intriguing; they can make your child stand out in positive ways. A girl named Sorrel won't be lost in a sea of Sorrels on Google searches and Facebook — but will have a strong, individuated identity. But there are caveats to choosing an unusual name as well — it's a mistake to try to make a name noticeable by concocting a bizarre spelling or choosing one with a problematic pronunciation or one that won't stand up when baby becomes an adult applying for a job.

This book will help you find that one fabulously unique name that's right for your unique child — and will help you avoid the pitfalls as well. Along with our picks is an index of the thousands of Nameberry names never in the Top 1000 in case you want to venture beyond our top picks. Here's a taste of the kinds of names you'll find inside:

- **Unusual names from nature** — such as Plum, Spruce, Wren, Clove and Tansy
- **Wonderful word names** — like Sonnet, Vesper, Temple and Verve
- **Untouristed place names** — from Vienna to Tennessee, Brighton to Rio
- **Brand new invented names that don't sound invented** — including Arissa, Calen, Jenessa, Garren, Arleigh and Brienna
- **Biblical finds** — uncommon Old and New Testament names like Tobiah, Phineas, Azaiah, Obadiah, Aram, Gallio and Joah
- **Great nicknames** — energetic choices such as Nika, Merce, Tilly, Zuzu, Bing and Bix
- **Exotic imports** — from the Welsh Rhonwen to the French Cosette to the Italian Vittorio to the Hebrew Varda
- **Blasts from the past** — like Gwendolen and Guinevere, Wallis and Vaughan, Amity and Clarity
- **Ancient treasures** — such as Artemis, Clio and Juno, Tristram and Tarquin
- **Literary namesakes** — Poe, Millay and Yeats
- **Irish surnames beyond Brady and Brody** — such as Donnelly, Gilby, Clooney and Sweeney

And lots, lots more. So dig in and find that very special name for your special child. And then be sure to check into Nameberry for even more!

GIRLS' NAMES

A

Abbott

Aramaic, Hebrew, "father"
This traditionally male surname name could find new life for girls thanks to its similarity to the popular Abby and Abigail.

Abelia

Hebrew, "sigh, breath"
This feminine form of Abel makes a distinctive alternative to the widely used Abigail.

Aberdeen

Scottish place-name
A much more modern choice than unfashionable Irish een-ending names like Noreen and Doreen.

Abilene

English from Hebrew, "grass"; also American place-name
Abilene is a rarely used place name, mentioned as such in the New Testament, that combines the cowboy spunk of the Texas city with the midwestern morality of the Kansas town where Dwight D. Eisenhower spent his boyhood. Abilene is a much more untrodden path to the nickname Abbie/Abbie than the Top 10 Abigail.

In 1857, Eliza Hersey named the frontier village of Abilene, Kansas, after a vast plain described in Luke's gospel.

Abilene is the title of a Sheryl Crow song, and the book *The Miraculous Journey of Edward Tulane* by Kate Dicamillo features a sweet character named Abilene.

Acadia

English from Greek, "idyllic place"
Acadia, the French name for Nova Scotia and the name of a gorgeous national park in Maine makes a fresh, rhythmic choice for your little girl.

The origin of the New World place name dates back to the sixteenth century borrowing of the ancient Greek name.

Adair

English and Scottish, "shallow place in a river near oaks"
This undiscovered unisex name has lots of flair. It was first noticed as a girl's name, starting in the 1980's, on the long-running daytime drama *Search for Tomorrow*, with the character Adair McCleary, who had ahead-of-their-time brothers named Hogan, Cagney and Quinn. But since Adair has yet to find many takers, it would make a fresh and appealing choice.

Adira

Hebrew, "strong"
Adira is one of those rare names that's both exotic and simple. Pronounced ah-DEER-ah, Adira is given to only a handful of girls in the US each year and could make a worthy substitute for such overexposed favorites as Ava and Ariana.

Adora

Latin, "adored"
A name that would lavish your child with adoration, a princess name — as in Princess Adora of *She-Ra: Princess of Power*.

Aeliana

ay-lee-AHN-ah
Latin, meaning unknown
This female form of the ancient Latin Aelian has an appealing sound, though kids might have a hard time handling that initial "ae" spelling. *The Annals of Aeliana* is a children's fantasy series by Ryan Watters.

Africa

Place name, various meanings
Most Africas today would be named for the continent, but the name actually existed in Scotland in medieval times, where there was a Celtic queen named Affrica. Africa has also been a Spanish name for girls since 1421. The church of

the Virgin "Nuestra Senora de Africa" is in Ceuta, the Spanish city she is Patron of, in North Africa.

There have been several other theories as to the origin of the name. Some believe it refers to the name of the ancient Berber people who inhabited North Africa, others believe Africa means "greyish" in reference to the color of sand, and yet another theory is that it is a Phoenician word meaning "colony," as Africa was once a colony of the Roman Empire. To complicate matters further, spelled Affrica, it is also used in Spanish-speaking countries, meaning "pleasant."

Africa has been a recorded name in the U.S. since the eighteenth century.

Afternoon
Word name
An early day name, found on slave rolls, and worthy of consideration today for someone seeking a truly unusual name.

Ailsa
AYL-suh

Scottish from Norse, "elf victory"
Ailsa is a traditional Scottish name related to a rocky island in the Firth of Clyde called Ailsa Craig. It might make an interesting alternative to the outdated Ashley or overly popular Ella, and could also be thought of as a relative of Elizabeth or Elsa.

Some other Ailsa relatives: Ailis, Ailse, Ailsha, Allasa, Elsha, Elshe.

Aisling
Irish, "dream, vision"
Aisling is currently a very popular name in Ireland. Pronounced variously as ASH-ling, ASH-lin or ash-LEEN, it was part of the revival of authentic Irish names in the twentieth century, and is now being sparingly used by US parents in place of the dated Ashley — though often spelled phonetically as Ashlyn or Ashlynn.

An aisling is a poetic genre that developed in late seventeenth century Ireland, a type of patriotic-romantic poetry in which Ireland is addressed as a beautiful woman.

Alanis

Female variation of Alan, "handsome, cheerful"

Singer Alanis Morissette made this twist famous. She was named for her father Alan, who is said to have spotted this version in a Greek newspaper. So far it has been pretty much a one-person name, but could make a distinctive update of Alana — especially with s-ending names making a comeback.

Alessia

Italian variation of Alexis, "defending warrior"

The lovely Alessia would provide a fresh spin on Alexa, Alexis or Alyssa — all becoming overused — but probably will often be mistaken for one of those more familiar names.

Alizabeth

Variation of Elizabeth, "pledged to God"

Unusual and attention-grabbing, but this unusual spelling also could make your child's life more complicated than it has to be.

Allegra

Italian, "joyous"

In music, the term allegro means "quickly, lively tempo," which makes this still-unusual and quintessential ballet dancer's name all the more appealing.

One of the most creative sounding of names, Allegra has been associated with the American prima ballerina Allegra Kent, and has been chosen as a first or middle name for their daughters by poets George Gordon, Lord Byron and Henry Wadsworth Longfellow, as well as by R. Buckminster Fuller and Donatella Versace.

Alouette

French, "lark"

Alouette is a sweet Gallic twist in the stylish bird name genre made familiar via the charming French children's song, *Alouette, gentile alouette.*

Amabel

Latin, "lovable"

Amabel is an older name than Annabel and a lot more distinctive. Amabel was a very common name in the twelfth and thirteen centuries, then was revived during the nineteenth century British fad for medieval names.

Its shortened form Mabel overtook the mama name early on.

Amadea

ah-mah-DAY-a

Latin, "God's beloved"

Amadea is a strong and musical feminine form of Amadeus, as in Mozart.

Amaia

Spanish, "high place"; Basque, "end"

This pretty and uncommon Spanish name is all but unheard of in this country. Amaya is a similar Japanese name meaning "night rain."

Amandine

French, diminutive of Amanda, "much-loved"

This fragrant, almond-scented name has hardly been heard in this country, which is a pity — we've loved it since John Malkovich used it for his now grown daughter.

A French diminutive of Amanda, it was the birth name of novelist George Sand — born Amandine Aurore Lucile — and currently ranks at Number 87 in France.

Of course, amandine is also a French culinary term for served with a garnish of almonds.

Amaryllis

Greek, "to sparkle"

If you're looking for a showier flower name than Lily, but staying in the same botanical family, you might consider Amaryllis, which is not as outre as it might at first sound. It was used in Greek poetry as the appellations of pure pastoral beauties; Amaryllis is the heroine of Virgil's epic poem *Ecologues*, after whom the flower was named. Other references are characters in the George Bernard Shaw play *Back to Methuselah* and *The Music Man*. James Bond-creator Ian Fleming had a half sister named Amaryllis Maris-Louise Fleming, who was a noted British cellist.

Ambrosia

Greek and Roman mythology name, "food of the gods"

Heavenly, if you like your names over the top.

Amethyst

Gem and Color name

As flower names become more exotic, so can gem names move beyond Ruby and Pearl to names like Topaz, Sapphire and Peridot. Amethyst, the purple birthstone for February, has never been in the Top 1000, but could have some appeal, joining similarly-hued Violet and Lilac.

In the M.M. Kaye children's novel *The Ordinary Princess*, the protagonist is Princess Amethyst Alexandra Augusta Araminta Adelaide Aurelia Anne of Phantasmorania — Amy for short — who has been given the "gift" of ordinariness.

Amity

Latin, "friendship"

Amity — what nicer gift to give your little girl than a name that signifies friendship and harmony? This virtue name is also more rhythmic and feminine than the single-syllable Hope, Faith, and Grace.

Amity is a neglected gem that could make a distinctive namesake for an Aunt Amy.

Amoret

Literary name

This lovely name from Spenser's *The Faerie Queene* is borne by a character who represents married love. A related unusual-yet-usable choice: Amabel.

Amoris

Latin, "love"

This Latin word for love is not traditionally used as a name, but why not? It's got a pretty sound and some distinctive flair. Variants Amori and Amorie can also be thought of as different spellings of Amory, which has a very different meaning and roots. Only downside: Sounds almost exactly like "amorous," meaning in the mood for love, which could provoke some adolescent teasing.

Amory

German, "industrious"

Amory is best known for the hero of Fitzgerald's 1920 *This Side of Paradise*, Princeton student Amory Blaine. Amory is in some danger of being borrowed by the girls, a la Avery. Alternate spellings Amori or Amorie also relate to the Latin word for love.

Andorra

European place name

Andorra is the pretty name of a pocket-sized princedom in the Pyrenees, noted for its skiing.

Andromeda

Greek mythology name, "advising like a man"

The beautiful daughter of Cassiopeia who, like her mother, literally became a star — the constellation that bears her name. It makes a dramatic and adventurous choice.

Anemone

ah-NEM-oh-nee

Flower name; Greek, "breath"

Anemone is a floral name taken from a mythological nymph who was turned into a flower by the wind; an interesting, if challenging, choice. Note that Anemone has *four* syllables.

Aniceta

Spanish from German, "unconquerable"

A delicate name with strong roots. Saint Anicetus was an ancient pope and martyr.

Anina

Aramaic, "let my prayer be answered"

This feminissima Italian palindrome name is rarely heard in the US, but could make an interesting namesake for an aunt or grandma Ann.

Annora

Latin, "honor"

Annora is a noble name, a distinctive twist on its most essential form: Honor. Other variations to explore include Honora and Nora.

Anouk

Dutch and French variation of Anna, "grace"

Anouk, made famous by French actress Anouk Aimée, is a singular name with a lovely sound. Anouk Aimée was born as Francoise, but adopted the first name of the character she played in her debut film.

Anouk, which is currently in the Top 20 in The Netherlands, was the name of the young daughter in the French film *Chocolat*. (Trivia tidbit: other interesting character names in that movie are Vianne, Roux and Dedou.) The Belgian supermodel spells her name Anouck Lepère.

Anouk is one of the most appealing of the An-starting names.

Anoushka

Russian, diminutive of Ann, "grace"

A lively, affectionate Olde World pet name wearing a baboushka and embroidered blouse.

Answer

Word name

An implied spiritual meaning makes this a plausible new name.

Antonella

Latin, "first born"

Antonella is an Italian version more feminine and exotic than Antonia. Antonina is a similarly appealing possibility, heard in Poland and Russia.

Anwen

Welsh, "very fair, beautiful"

Anwen is one of the simplest and best of the classic Welsh girls' names, more unusual than Bronwen but with the same serene feel.

Aphra

Hebrew, variation of Aphrah, "dust"

Aphra would make an interesting choice — especially since it's the name of the first professional female writer in English, the seventeenth century's Aphra Behn. Born in 1640, she was a prolific dramatist of the English Restoration.

Aphra was originally a name for a woman from Africa that eventually became a given name, and was borne by several Roman saints. It can also be spelled Afra.

Apollonia

Greek, Feminine variation of Apollo, Greek sun god.

This name of a third century Christian martyr has an exotic, appealing feel in the modern world. It first came to American attention via Prince's love interest in the film *Purple Rain*. Apollonia is the name of a character in John Steinbeck's novel, *The Pearl*.

Apple

Nature name

Apple made international headlines when Gwyneth Paltrow chose this wholesome fruit name for her daughter. Many have called it ridiculous, but we have to admit, we find it kinda cute. Rocker Bob Geldof named one of his daughters Peaches; Banana Yoshimoto is a hipster writer. Another choice in this genre is the luscious Plum, though for different reasons, neither Prune nor Cherry will fly.

Arbor

Nature name

Arbor is an original unisex tree-related choice we're sure to hear more of. Highly unusual now, Arbor takes its place alongside other new arborial names ranging from the mighty Oak (or Oakley) to the more delicate Birch to the more flowery Juniper, Acacia, and Hazel.

Arcadia

Greek, "region offering peace and contentment"

Arcadia, a name for an unspoiled paradise, makes an attractive secular alternative to Neveah. For parents who want an unusual name with a friendlier nickname, Arcadia has the advantage of cute Cady.

Arcelia

Spanish, "treasure chest"

Arcelia is an undiscovered Spanish treasure worth considering. Exotic yet friendly to the English-speaking tongue, Arcelia combines the trendiness of an *A* name with the delicacy of Celia.

Argenta

Latin, "silvery"

More modern and exotic than Silver, Argenta is one of the few mineral/metal-related names.

Ariadne

Greek, "most holy"

This name of the Cretan goddess of fertility is most popular now as the more melodic Ariana, but Ariadne has possibilities of its own.

Artemis

Greek mythology name

Artemis is the ancient goddess of the moon and the hunt, equivalent to the Roman Diana, but a fresher and more distinctive, if offbeat, choice.

Artemis was the twin sister of Apollo, one of the twelve deities who lived on Mount Olympus. She is also the goddess of children and all weak things, and features in three of the fifth century plays of Euripides.

Arwen

Welsh, "noble maiden"

Arwen is well known as princess of the Elves in Tolkien's *Lord of the Rings*: a lovely name with an authentic Welsh ring. If you love Arwen, you might also want to consider Anwen, Bronwen, and Rhonwen.

Ashby

English, "ash tree farm"

Ashby is an Ashley substitute with a slightly more unisex feel; it was picked for her daughter by TV host Nancy O'Dell.

Aster

English, flower name

This is a fresh new addition to the botanical list; comedian Gilbert Gottfried made it a real bouquet when he named his daughter Lily Aster. And the name of the little girl on television's *Dexter* sounds like Aster, but is actually spelled Astor.

Atlanta

Place-name

Georgia and Savannah are popular, but Atlanta is just entering the baby-name map. Atalanta takes it mythological.

Auberon

English from German, "noble, bearlike"

With the growing popularity for girls of such names as Aubrey and Audrey, Auberon feels like a fresh and viable option.

Auburn

Color name

With its rich aural relation to names like Aubrey and Audrey, this color name could be the next Amber, or Scarlett.

Auden

English, "old friend"

A softly poetic surname name, associated with poet W.H., Auden is enjoying quiet but marked fashion status. It was chosen for his daughter by Noah Wyle and is definitely one to watch.

Aurelia

Latin, "the golden one"

Aurelia is the shimmering female form of the Roman classic Aurelius, very common in the Roman Empire but rarely heard in modern America. The name of several minor early saints, Aurelia has the right sound, feel and meaning to rise again. Aurora and Oriana are Aurelia cousins you might also want to consider. Aurelia was the name of the mothers of both Julius Caesar and the writer Sylvia Plath.

Austen

Shortened form of Augustine, "venerable"; literary surname

While Austin is a popular boys' name, this spelling, honoring novelist Jane, is more girlish.

Avalon

Celtic, "island of apples"

Avalon, an island paradise of Celtic myth and Arthurian legend (and also the capital of the California island of Catalina) makes a heavenly first name. Actress Rena Sofer used it for her daughter — it's an attractive and interesting way of elaborating on Ava.

Aveline

French cognate of Hazel, "the hazelnut tree

Aveline is a name that's long been an obscure cousin of more widely-used choices, but may come into its own riding the tail of the megapopular Ava. Aveline's roots, however, are not the same as Ava's bird-related origins but connect with the ancient Roman place name Avella, which means "filbert" or "hazelnut."

Aveline is different enough to sound distinct, but be warned: You will probqbly forever be explain that no, it's not Adeline, not Evelyn, and so on.

Averil

English, "boar battle"

An ancient female saint's name, also spelled Averill, with different roots than either Ava or April. Though it resembles both those more fashionable favorites, it's fresher and more appealing than either, we think.

Aviva

Hebrew, "springlike, fresh, dewy"

Aviva is vivacious and memorable, a fresh spin on the Vivian and Vivienne names that have been getting more popular since Angelina and Brad chose one for their twin daughter. Another A-beginning palindrome name: Aziza.

Ayelet

eye-YELL-it or EYE-leht

Hebrew, "deer, gazelle"

Ayelet is an unusual — and somewhat challenging — Israeli name familiar thanks to sometimes controversial Jerusalem-born novelist-essayist Ayelet Waldman.

Well used in Israel, the name was taken from the phrase 'ayelet hashachar', meaning 'gazelle of dawn', the morning star.

Other related Hebrew choices with the same meaning are Aya and Ayala.

Aziza

uh-ZEE-zah

Hebrew, "mighty"; Arabic and Swahili, "precious"

Aziza is a zippy palindromic choice. Aziza also means "precious" in Swahili and Arabic. All in all, an attractive and interesting choice. A Turkish variation is Azize.

Azure

Color name

Azure is a colorful choice for a blue-eyed child. Other blue-toned color name possibilities: Indigo, Cerulean, and Blue itself.

B

Bathsheba

Hebrew, "daughter of an oath"

Popular with the Puritans, this name of the shrewd and beautiful wife of King David and daughter of King Solomon could be a bit of a load for a modern girl to carry.

Bathsheba is the name of the central character in the Thomas Hardy novel *Far from the Madding Crowd*.

Bay

Vietnamese, "seventh child," nature name

One of the most usable of the pleasant, newly adopted nature/water names (like Lake and Ocean), especially in middle position.

Baylor

English, "horse trainer"

Baylor is a possible occupational alternative to the tired Taylor, especially for a horse lover.

Beah

Short form of Beatrice, "bringer of happiness"

A rarely seen member of the Beatrice clan, with its own distinctive charm.

Bechet

French surname

Naming babies for personal heroes is the cool contemporary trend followed by Woody Allen when he honored New Orleans jazz clarinetist Sidney Bechet in his daughter's name — adding the middle name Dumaine after a cornet player who was another of his musical heroes. Bechet has a nice, catchy Gallic feel.

Bellamy

English and Irish from French, "fine friend"

Bellamy is emerging as an up-and-coming girls' name, a surname-y riff on the super-popular Bella series of name. While the Bella connection makes Bellamy sound trendier and more popular than it really is, we see the name rising through the ranks for girls in coming years.

Benedetta

Latin, "blessed"

The saintly Italian form of the saintly Latin Benedicta.

Benilde

ben-NIL-dee

French variation of Latin, "good"

The strong and unusual name of a medieval (male) saint and a contemporary (female) novelist, Benilde Little.

Berry

Nature name

With the recent arrival of fruit names like Apple and Plum, this more traditional example, symbolic of fertility, might rise in popularity. Photographer Berry Berenson was born Berinthia. And…inspired by us… a babyberry was actually named Berry!

Bertille

French, "heroine, bright maiden"

The name of a medieval French saint, similar to Sally Field's name, Bertrille, on the old *The Flying Nun* sitcom, leading some to expect the word "Sister" in front of it.

Bijou

bee-zhoo

French, "jewel"

Bijou is a name that lives up to its definition — a real jewel. Warning: not unheard of on poodles' dog collars. Actress Bijou Phillips is its best known bearer. It can also be spelled Bijoux.

Birgit

Scandinavian variation of Brighid, "strength"

Birgit is pronounced with a hard 'g' and is one of the many international versions of the Irish Bridget. Birgit Nilsson was a celebrated Swedish operatic soprano.

Blaine

Irish, "slender, angular"

She's the bff of Blair, Blake, and Brooke who shops at Bergdorf's, Bonwits and Bendel's.

Bliss

English word name

This is a name only for parents positive their daughter won't ever have a tantrum. Same goes for Merry, Joy and Gay.

Blue

Color name

Blue is suddenly in the spotlight, as the unusual color name chosen by Beyonce and Jay-Z for their baby girl. Blue is also a starbaby middle name du jour, used for both sexes in different spellings and forms, from John Travolta and Kelly Preston's Ella Bleu to Alicia Silverstone's Bear Blu. Blue is the heroine of the trendy novel *Special Topics in Calamity Physics*.

Blythe

English, "free spirit, happy, carefree"

Blythe embodies a cheerful, carefree spirit and could be the next Brooke. Other light-hearted names for girls: Felicity, Hilary.

Branwen

Celtic, "blessed raven"

This is an attractive Celtic mythological name, popular in Wales and a cousin of the better known Bronwyn. In Welsh muthology, Branwen was turned into a bird.

Brennan

Irish, "descendent of the sad one"

Poised for popularity, Brennan is an Irish last name soft enough to borrow from the boys.

Briar

English, "a thorny patch"

Fairy-tale memories of "Sleeping Beauty" inspire some parents to call their daughters Briar Rose.

Bride

BREE-da

Irish, "strength"

Technically a pet form of Brigid and very commonly heard in Ireland, but pronunciation problems complicate Bride as a name choice in America.

Bronwen

Welsh, "white breast"

Bronwen is widespread in Wales, but still rare enough here to sound somewhat exotic — we think Bronwen is a real winner. (Note: the Bronwyn spelling is strictly for males in its native land.)

Bronwen Morgan was the lovely heroine of the classic novel and movie *How Green Was My Valley*. In Welsh mythology, Bronwen is the daughter of Llyr, the god of the sea.

Bryony

Brian-nee

Latin flower name, "to sprout"

Bryony is an unusually strong plant name — the bryony is a wild climbing vine with green flowers — that caught on in the UK before sprouting here. The name of the young character in the Ian McEwan novel *Atonement* is spelled Briony.

Bryony sounds a lot fresher than the now dated Brittany. Pronunciation is like Brian with an ee at the end.

C

Caia

Latin, feminine variation of Caius, "to rejoice"

Caia Caecilia was the Roman Goddess of fire and women. The name Caia would make a truly fresh alternative to the flagging Maya, with which it rhymes.

Cairo

Place name

Model Beverly Peele put the exotic name Cairo on the map when she chose it for her daughter; it's much less faddish sounding than closer place-names like Dallas and Dakota.

Calico

English word name

A word name with the fashionable *o*-ending that has associations with both the homespun fabric and the mottled cat. Alice Cooper named his daughter Calico decades ago.

Calixta

Greek, "most beautiful"

Calista Flockhart may have made her variation of this beautiful Greek name familiar to modern Americans, but the even-edgier x version was the name of an earlier feminist heroine: a character in Kate Chopin's *The Storm*.

Calliope

ka-LYE-oh-pee

Greek mythology name, "beautiful voice"

Calliope is the name of the muse of epic poetry — and also the musical instrument on the merry-go-round. Bold and creative, it would not be the easiest name for a girl lacking such qualities.

Callista

Greek, "most beautiful"

Calista Flockhart spotlighted this lovely Greek name that has a long future in the English-speaking world. Kallista is another spelling; Calixta and Calixto are related.

Calypso

Greek, "she who hides"

This hyper-rhythmic name has two evocative references. In Greek mythology, she was an islnd nymph, a daughter of Atlas, who delayed Odysseus from returning home. It is also a genre of West Indian music, originating in Trinadad and Tobago and largely popularized in the states by Harry Belafonte.

Calypso was the name of Jacques-Yves Costeau's research ship — and would make a highly dramatic and musical choice.

Camellia

Flower name

Camellia is an exotic flower name with distinct roots related to the Camille/Camila group and has varied associations to the moon, wealth and perfection. It could be a floral replacement for Amelia.

Cameo

Word name

This evocative term for a stone or shell carved in relief could make a striking first name for a girl, though she would have a starring role in her story, rather than a cameo.

Capucine

French, "cowled monk"

Capucine was a sexy French actress half a century ago that is a tres chic baby name in Paris right now.

Carys

Ka-RISS

Welsh, "love"

Common in Wales, this name was introduced to America when Welsh-born Catherine Zeta-Jones and husband Michael Douglas chose it for their daughter in 2003. It didn't come into use in Wales until the late nineteenth century.

Cassia

Botanical name; Greek, "cinnamon"

Cassia is one of the rare names that's truly unusual yet has a stylish feel. Cassia has the added attraction of the sweet smell of cinnamon; a cassia tree or bush, which has yellow flowers, produces a spice that can be a substitute for cinnamon. We predict Cassia will become much more popular along with her brother names Cassian and Cassius. Keziah, the Biblical equivalent, is also due for rediscovery, while Kassia is another, Kardashian-style spelling.

Cassiopeia

kass-ee-OH-pee-uh

Greek mythology name

Cassiopeia, the name of a mythological mother who became a stellar constellation, is challenging but intriguing, and has all those softening Cass nicknames available. With the rise of other otherworldly and mythical choices, from Apollo to Jupiter to Juno, Cassiopeia may just feel more possible for mortals now than ever before in its long history.

Cerelia

Latin, "relating to springtime"

Cerelia is a melodic and unusual choice, perfect for a child born in April or May. Another version is Cerella.

Charmian

Greek, "joy"

This name was used by Shakespeare (who got it from Plutarch) in *Antony and Cleopatra* for one of the attendants of the Egyptian queen. An interesting possibility, it is heard occasionally in the UK, even less frequently in the US.

Chiara

kee-AHR-a

Italian, "light, clear"

Chiara is a lovely and romantic Italian name that's familiar but not widely used here: a real winner. You might consider Chiara instead of Claire, Clara, Cara, or even Keira.

Santa Chiara, Anglicized as St. Clara, was a follower of Saint Francis of Assisi.

Two members of European cinema royalty, Catherine Deneuve and Marcello Mastroianni, named their now grown daughter Chiara. Chiara currently ranks Number 6 in Italy and is also well used in Switzerland, Germany and Austria.

Christabel

Latin/French, "fair Christian"

Though Isabel is a smash hit, Christabel still hasn't been fully embraced. It was originally popularized in England via the Coleridge poem *Christabel* ("whom her father loves so well") and was given to the poet's granddaughter. Christabel Pankhurst was a famous UK suffragist.

Chrysanthemum

Greek, "gold flower"

One of the rarest of the flower names, that of the blossom celebrated in Japan as a symbol of the sun and a possible object of meditation.

Chrysanthemum is the title of a 1991 children's picture book by the American writer and illustrator Kevin Henkes. The plot deals with a young mouse named Chrysanthemum, who loves her name until classmates tease her about it.

Cia

Diminutive of Cynthia, "of the moon"

What's Cia short for? Cynthia or most any other *C*-name. Stylish in its sleek Mia-Nia minimalist feel, but may remind some of the Central Intelligence Agency.

Ciel

see-EL

French, "sky"

This simple yet evocative French word name was chosen for her daughter by model Niki Taylor. While Ciel may be pronounced in French with two syllables, many will pronounce it as "seal" and there may be confusion with Celia and sister Ceil.

Cimmaron

Place name

Cimmaron is an alternate spelling of Cimarron, a Great Plains city and river made famous by the Edna Ferber novel; it has a nice western feel. Cimmaron or more properly Cimarron is one of those vintage literary names, like Atticus and Scout, that may finally come into its own.

Circe

SUR-see

Greek, "bird"

In Greek myth, Circe, daughter of Helios, the sun, was a sorceress living on the island of Aeaea, who could turn men into animals with her magic wand, which is just what she did to Odysseus's crew in Homer's *Odyssey,* transforming them into swine. All was forgiven, however, as Circe and Odysseus later had a child together — Telegonus.

The name and legend have appeared in countless forms, from short stories by Julio Cortazar and Philip K. Dick to *Harry Potter* to Toni Morrison's *Song of Solomon* to films to DC comics to a dance by Martha Graham.

So is Circe's seductive legend too powerful for a modern little girl to carry? Your call.

Citron

French, "lemon"

A Gallic twist on a word or nature name, which has a nice lemony feel.

Clancy

Irish, "red-haired warrior"

Irish surnames are hot, and this one can successfully cross the line to work for girls, replacing the outdated Casey.

Clarity

Virtue name

Clarity is one of the lightest of the newly discovered virtue names, with a bit of three-syllable sparkle, old-fashioned charm and a clear vision for the future. Clarity is a very desirable quality in this confusing world and it also, unlike some other newly coined word names, has real meaning and history as a name.

Clarity is preferable to Charity and definitely to Chastity, with the possibility of Clare as a short form.

Clea

CLAY-uh

Literary name

An attractive and unusual name that may be a variation of Cleo, Clea was possibly invented by Lawrence Durrell for a character in his *Alexandria Quartet*.

Clelia

Latin, "famous"

The obscure yet not unappealing name of a legendary heroine of Rome. The ancient Clelia escaped an Etruscan invader by swimming across the Tiber River.

Clemency

Virtue name

One of the rarest of virtue names, Clemency could come back along with the more familiar Puritan virtue names, like Hope and Faith. It has a rhythmic three-syllable sound, and offers a more virtuous alternative to the more popular Clementine.

Clemence is the medieval French form, also heard occasionally in the UK. Writer Clemence Dane was born Winifred Ashton.

Clemmie makes a cute nickname.

Clia

Invented literary name

Clia could be seen as a variation of Clea (probably another invented literary name), or the creation of L. Frank Baum for a mermaid Princess character in one of his *Oz* books. Offers a similar choice to Cleo vs Clio.

Clothilde

French from German, "famous in battle"

Pronounced klo-TEELD, this name is well used in France, but rarely heard here; it has a chic and sophisticated air.

Cloud

Nature name

This kind of plainspoken nature name (think River and Sunshine) may still carries a whiff of the hippie, but this one has a nice, airy feel.

Clover

Flower name

Clover is a charming, perky choice if you want to move beyond hothouse blooms like Rose and Lily, and it's recently become a new celeb favorite, chosen by both Neal McDonough and Natasha Gregson Wagner, who used it to honor her mother, Natalie Wood, one of whose most iconic films was *Inside Daisy Clover*.

Clover also has a long association with good luck, via the four-leaf clover, and through the shamrock symbol of Ireland. It first came to wide notice via a couple of soap opera characters. In the movie *The Good Shepherd*, Angelina Jolie's character is called Clover — but her birth name was actually Margaret.

Coco

Spanish and French pet name

Coco came to prominence as the nickname of the legendary French designer Chanel (born Gabrielle) and has lately become a starbaby favorite, initially chosen by Courteney Cox for her daughter Coco Riley in 2004. At first it was the kind of name that the press loves to ridicule, but we predict Coco's heading for more broad acceptance and even popularity.

Columba

Latin, "dove"

Columba is an early saint's name that rhumbas to a modern beat. While the original St. Columba is male, the name sounds more appropriate for a girl in the modern world. Leave variations Colm and Callum for the boys.

Comfort

Word name

This Puritan virtue name may be unstylish, but it is also sympathetic and appealing in these largely uncomfortable times.

Connelly

Irish, "love, friendship"

Connelly is a rollicking and rare example of the popular surname genre that may work even better for girls. A huge update on Colleen.

Constantina

Latin, female variation of Constantinus, "constant, unchanging"
Constantina is a pretty, feminissima, if lengthy, variation on the Constance theme. The fourth century Constantina, also known as Constantia and Constantiana, was the eldest daughter of Roman Emperor Constantine the Great and his second wife Fausta, daughter of Emperor Maximian. Constantina received the title of Augusta by her father, and is venerated as a saint; in English she is also known as Saint Constance.

Constanza

Italian, feminine form of Constantine, "constant, unchanging"
This version adds some Italian flair to the somewhat stolid Constance.

Cordis

Latin, "of the heart"
Cordis is an unusual and substantial unisex choice.

Corin

Latin, "spear"
Corin is a Shakespearean male name that could easily be adapted for a girl, making a strong update for Corinne or Karen.

Corisande

Greek, "chorus-singer"
Corisande is a very unusual, haunting choice, with the aura of medieval romance — it is found in early Spanish romantic tales, arriving in the English-speaking world in the nineteenth century

'La belle Corisande' was the poetic name applied to Diane de Poitiers, the beautiful and powerful mistress of King Henry II — Henri of Navarre — of France.

Lady Corisande is the leading character in Benjamin Disraeli's 1870 novel *Lothair*, and, more recently, was seen in Annabel Davis-Goff's novel *This Cold Country*.

Cosette

French, female version of Nicolas, "victorious people"; also a nickname, "little thing"
Cosette is best known as the heroine of *Les Miserables*. In the Victor Hugo novel, Cosette was the nickname given to the girl named Euphrasie by her mother.

Despite the popularity of *Les Mis* the musical, the name was given to only seventy-five girls in 2011, but this may change with the wide exposure of the movie. Cosette would make a sweet if coquettish French choice.

Cosima

KO-see-mah

Greek, feminine variation of Cosmo, "universe"

Cosima, the kind of elegant and exotic name the British upper classes love to use for their daughters, will almost certainly come into wider use here after being chosen by two high-profile celebs in the same month — cool couple Sofia Coppola and Thomas Mars as well as supermodel Claudia Schiffer. It was used earlier by celebrity chef Nigella Lawson, while the male form, Cosimo, was given to the son of Marissa Ribisi and Beck.

The most famous Cosima in history had strong musical ties — Cosima Wagner was the daughter of composer Franz Liszt and the wife of composer Richard Wagner. Cosima is well used in Germany, Italy and Greece.

Cressida

KRESS-i-da

Greek, "gold"

Cressida is a pretty mythological and Shakespearean heroine name much better known in Britain than it is here — an imbalance the adventurous baby namer might want to correct. For although the Trojan heroine of that name in the tale told by Boccaccio, then Chaucer, then Shakespeare, didn't have the greatest reputation — she was faithless to Troilus and broke his heart — the name today sounds fresh, crisp and creative.

Crimson

Color name

Crimson could be a possible competitor for Scarlett's success, though it's lacking that *Gone With the Wind* charm.

Curran

Irish, "hero, champion"

Curran is a curry-flavored Irish surname-y name that could work as well for girls as boys. Curran can be a fresher spin on the *Twilight*-inflected Cullen.

Cyan

Color name

Cyan is an attractive color name, but for a girl, better go all the way to Cyane, the name of a Sicilian nymph who lived in a blue pool.

Cybele

si-BELL

Greek, "the mother of all gods"

Cybele, the name of a Greek goddess of fertility, health, and nature, would unfortunately and undoubtedly be confused with Sybil.

D

Dacia

Latin place-name

Dacia is an ancient place name — it was in Eastern Europe — as lacy as Dacey, but more substantial.

Daffodil

Flower name

Yes, though it seems so extreme,girls were actually sometimes given this name a century ago; now it is so uncommon it would make a strong springtime statement. Biggest obstacle: the nickname Daffy.

The daffodil is the national flower of Wales, and in the language of flowers it symbolizes both respect and unrequited love.

But if this all seems too much, you could just go with Daisy.

Dalila

Swahili, "gentle"

A rhythmic name that sounds similar to Delilah and is heard in several different languages: Hebrew, Spanish, Tanzanian, and Swahili.

Damara

Greek, "gentle girl"

This name of an ancient fertility goddess is associated with the month of May and could make a pretty, unusual choice for a springtime baby. Damaris is a similar possibility.

Dancer

Word name

A word name that's appealing when applied to a person boogying or doing ballet; a different story in the context of Santa's reindeer.

Danya

Hebrew, "judgment of God," Russian, diminutive of Daniel

An energetic name with an ethnic, embroidered feel.

Day

Word name

A bright and optimistic middle name choice.

December

Word name

Cooler than April, May, or June, but also a tad icy.

Delancey

French, "from Lancey"

This is an energetic dance of an Irish surname, great for both genders. Could also be spelled Delancy.

Delphi

Greek place name

An interesting unisex possibility, with an air of mystery connected to the Delphic Oracle, the most important oracle in ancient Greece; it was also a major site for the worship of the god Apollo.

Destry

English variation of French, "warhorse"

This was the male hero's last name in the classic film *Destry Rides Again,* but in today's anything-goes naming climate, nobody blinked when the Steven Spielbergs picked it for their daughter. A real winner.

Dharma

Sanskrit, "truth"

In Buddhism, Dharma embodies the basic principles of cosmic existence, making it a fitting name for the hippyish character on the sitcom *Dharma & Greg,* whose middle name was Freedom. Students of Beat literature will be familiar with the name via part of the title of a Kerouac novel, Dharma Bums.

Diablo

Spanish, "devil"

Diablo Cody, self-named (she's really Brook Busey) screenwriter of *Juno*, singlehandedly helped popularize not just her heroine's name and her own but all o-ending names for girls. You don't need us to tell you that it takes a brave parent, in every way, to name a baby Diablo.

Diantha

Greek, "divine flower"

Diantha, a mythological flower of Zeus, is a melodious and more unusual cousin of Diana, heard most often in The Netherlands. Some similar choices: Diandra and Dianthe.

Doe

English, "a female deer"

Doe is a soft and gentle-eyed middle name possibility and, like Fawn, one of the few animal names open to girls. *The Ballad of Baby Doe* is a modern American opera based on the story of Elizabeth McCourt Tabor, known as Baby Doe.

So yes, use the sweet Doe as a middle name for your daughter — just not if her first name will be Jane.

Dominica

Italian, feminine variation of Dominic, "belonging to the Lord"

Fashionably Continental, much fresher than Dominique. Dominica can be spelled any number of ways, from Dominika to Domenica, but we prefer this version.

Domino

Latin, "lord, master"

One of those ultimate cool-girl names, played by Keira Knightley in a movie about a supermodel-turned-bounty hunter, but kids might associate it with the game. High profile British designer India Hicks used it for her daughter.

Doon

Scottish surname

Photographer Diane Arbus named her daughter Doon, inspired by the sand dunes she walked among when pregnant.

Dory

French, "golden," or diminutive of Dorothy, "gift of God"

A Dorothy nickname name with a measure of nostalgic charm. Kids will associate it with the funny fish character voiced by Ellen DeGeneris in the Pixar animated instant classic *Finding Nemo*.

Dree

Diminutive of Andrea, feminine form of Andrew, "strong and manly"

This unique one-syllable name was added to the mix by Mariel Hemingway for her now grown daughter; it could make a distinctive middle name or Bree substitute.

E

East

Word name

North and West are easier on the ear, but this works fine if it has some significance for your family. Could be lengthened to Easton.

Edda

Norse, "poetry"

This Old Norse name has a lovely meaning but not too appealing a sound when removed from her native habitat. If you're looking for a girl namesake name for Ed, try Edwina instead.

Edwige

ed-WEEG

French from German Hedwig, "war"

Haitian writer Edwidge Danticat highlighted this sophisticated, chignon-wearing choice for literate parents.

Eilish

AY-leesh

Anglicized variation of Eilis, Irish form of Hebrew Elizabeth, "pledged to God"

An unusual name with both biblical and Irish roots. The Eilis form was popular in medieval times, and is still heard in modern Ireland; Eilish is more pleasing to the ear.

Electra

Greek, "shining, bright"

Though the tragedies of the Greeks and Eugene O'Neill that used this name are filled with incest and murder, Electra is still a brilliant choice. Isabella Rossellini chose the gentler Italian verson, Elletra, for her now grown daughter.

Eleonara

Italian, German, Dutch, and Polish version of Eleanor, "bright, shining one"
The usual form of Eleonara is Eleanora, with each syllable pronounced, but transposing, adding, or subtracting a vowel or syllable here or there works fine and adds to the exotic, feminine spin on a solid name.

Eliane

Variation of Eliana, Hebrew, "my God has answered"; Latin from Greek, "sun"
Eliane is a melodic name with the very fashionable El- beginning. Lovely and lilting as it is, be aware that there are many El- variations around these days, and little girls called Ellie as a result.

Elisabetta

Italian variation of Elizabeth, "pledged to God"
This version softens, feminizes, and glamorizes the long-time favorite. A fresh way to honor Grandma Betty. Elizabetta is a variation.

Elizabella

Combination of Eliza and Bella
Elizabella is a much more obscure smoosh than sisters Isabella and Annabelle, but the megapopularity of Isabella may give this unusual combo name a boost.

Ellery

English, "island with elder trees"
In the past few years Ellery has gone from middle-aged male detective to a plausible girls' name, a la Hillary.

Ellington

English place-name and surname, "Ellis' town"
Ellington's popularity may be inspired by jazz great Duke, but the name is used slightly more often for girls today, perhaps because of its trendy El- beginning. Like a host of other El- names, from the familiar Ella to Eleanor to the exotic Elodie and Elula, Ellington carries the popular Ellie nickname.

Ellison

English, "son of Ellis"
Updates Allison — which everyone will misunderstand it as. But definitely another fresh spin on the Ellie and Alissa names.

Elowen

Cornish, "elm"

Elowen is a lovely nature name from Cornwell that can be used for girls or boys. Not heard much before the twentieth century, when the Cornish language was revived, it blends well with the Welsh 'wen'-ending names and the trendy El-beginning names, and has a pleasant, evocative sound.

Elowen does not have the long history of other Cornish names such as Kerenza and Tamsyn: it was officially recognized under the European charter as recently as 2002.

Elspeth

Scottish variation of Elizabeth, "pledged to God"

One of those names that never quite made it out of the British Isles, but possesses a winningly childlike charm. Elspeth was used by Sir Walter Scott for several of his female characters.

Elula

Hebrew, female form of Elul, month name

Elula, female derivation of Elul, the name of the sixth month on the Hebrew calendar, was used by Isla Fisher and Sacha Baron Cohen for their second daughter. The couple kept their unusual choice under wraps for several months, perhaps to get a head start on the hordes of fans who might adopt the fashionable-yet-unusual double-l name for their own. Reminiscent of Eulalia, the stylish pick of Marcia Gay Harden for her daughter. Lula, Lulu, or Lu could be short forms.

Eluned

el-LOOND or el-EEN-ed

Welsh, "idol, image"

Exotic and mysterious, Eluned's beauty and intelligence were legendary in Welsh legend; she was the handmaiden of the Lady of the Fountain in a Welsh Arthurian romance, who had a magic ring that made the wearer invisible.

Embeth

Combination of Emma and Beth

South African-raised actress Embeth Davidtz added this unique name to the mix. Perfect if you can't decide between Emma and Elizabeth.

Embry

English surname, "flat-topped hill"

Though Embry became famous as the name of a boy werewolf in *Twilight*, we think its Em- beginning and -y ending make it perfectly appropriate for a girl. You might consider it as an alternative to Emma, Emily, or Aubrey. Embry or Embury is an established English surname.

Emmanuelle

French, feminine variation of Emanuel, "God is with us"

The female version of Emanuel could become more prominent, though for some it still carries a steamy image dating back to a then sensationally erotic French film.

Emmeline

French form of German Amelina, "work"

Emmeline, also spelled with one 'm', is an Emma relative and Emily cousin that is destined for greater use in the wake of the megapopularity of those two names. A recommended Nameberry fave.

A popular medieval name, Emmeline was introduced to Britain by the Normans. It appeared as a character in *Uncle Tom's Cabin*, and is famous in Britain as the name of the illustrous suffragette, Emmeline Pankhurst. Way back in 1980, it was the name of young Brooke Shield's innocent character in *The Blue Lagoon*.

Eponine

French literary name

Eponine is attracting new notice via the movie of *Les Miserables*, based on the book by Victor Hugo. Eponine is the spoiled daughter of Cosette's foster parents whose name, according to the story, was lifted by her mother from a romance novel. As in a romance, Eponine redeems herself by becoming a martyr to love.

Engracia

Spanish from Latin, "endowed with God's grace"

An exotic and charming alternative to the overused Grace.

Eos

Greek, "dawn"

Eos — that's pronounced with a short e like eros without the r — is the Greek Titan of the dawn. Any ancient name with a sleek modern feel has definite revival possibilities. Eos could be an inventive way to honor grandma Dawn.

Etain

Irish, "jealousy"

The Etain of Irish mythology was a beautiful fairy turned into a fly (or in some versions, a butterfly), by a jealous queen. The insect Etain fell into a glass of milk and was swallowed by yet another queen, then reborn as a beautiful maiden. The name Etain not only survives but is popular in modern Ireland. With the transatlantic success of Aiden, which is resembles, Etain may well have a future in the U.S.

Evan

Welsh variation of John, "the Lord is gracious"

Evan is a boys' favorite brought to the girls' side by talented young actress Evan Rachel Wood.

Eyre

Literary name and Old Norse, "gravel bank river"

This lovely name — Eyre sounds just like air — is best-known as the surname of eponymous Bronte heroine Jane, and would make an appealing and distinctive middle name for the child of fans of that book. While the surname Eyre is found mainly in England, its origins are Norse and it's thought to derive from Norse settlers.

F

Fabiana

Italian and Spanish feminine variation of Fabian, "bean grower"

The fashion for elaborate girly-girl names, especially those that end with -ella or -ana, has put this distinctive Latin favorite into play.

Fable

Word name

Fable, like Story, is a word name with real potential, combining enchanted tale-telling with a moral edge.

Farrell

Irish, "courageous"

Farrell is usually considered a boy's name, though the soft sound of this Irish surname makes it perfectly appropriate for a girl, reminiscent of Farrah.

Federica

Italian, feminine variation of Frederick, "peaceful ruler"

Federica is the Latin version of Frederica, one of those formerly stuffy female names — think Josephine and Eleanor — that feels fresh and elegant again. And Federica has more energy without that first r.

Fenella

Celtic, "white-shouldered one"

The engaging Scottish Fenella, the heroine of a Sir Walter Scott novel, is, though scarcely heard in this country, much more user-friendly than some of the Irish versions.

Fia

Irish, diminutive of Fiachna, "raven"

A pleasantly light and distinctive possible alternative to Mia.

Finch

English word and nature name, "to swindle"

Bird name possibility, though it perhaps feels a bit pinched.

Finula

Irish Gaelic, "white shoulders"

This phonetic spelling of the Gaelic Fionnuala (which also has many spelling variations) is sometimes rendered as Finola or Finella.

Fiorella

Italian, "little flower"

Feminine, floral, and rarely enough heard here to be exotic.

Flannery

Irish, diminutive of Flanna, "red-haired"

Long before the vogue of using Irish surnames for girls, writer Flannery O'Connor gave this one some visibility. It has a warm (flannelly) feel and the currently popular three-syllable ee-ending sound.

Fleur

French, "flower"

Fleur is a generic, delicate flower name that runs the risk of sounding a bit precious. Fleur emigrated into the English-speaking world when John Galsworthy bestowed it on one of the Forsytes in his celebrated saga. More recently, there was Fleur Delacoeur,a French witch in *Harry Potter.*

Flynn

Irish, "son of the red-haired one"

A winning last-name-first Celtic choice, Flynn is still mostly used for boys, such as the son of Orlando Bloom and Miranda Kerr. Though, as with other Irish surname names, from Quinn to Flannery to Makenna, there's no reason it couldn't work for girls.

Forsythia

Flower name

This yellow harbinger of spring bloom was named for Scottish botanist William Forsyth, and is even more unusual than such exotic species as Acacia and Azalea.

France

Place name

This geographic name has lots of Gallic elan. France Nuyen is French-Vietnamese actress who starred in the Broadway hit *The World of Suzie Wong*.

Franny

Latin, diminutive of Frances, "from France or free man"

If Frances and Fran are too serious for you, and Fanny too saucy, you might like Franny, still identified by some with J. D. Salinger's *Franny and Zooey* stories.

Freesia

Flower name

A really exotic, free-feeling flower name for the parent who wants to move far,far beyond Rose and Daisy.

Freya

FRAY-a

Norse, "a noble woman"

Freya, the name of the Norse goddess of love, beauty and fertility, has long been popular in the UK but just beginning to be appreciated here. Freya could make a possible namesake for an ancestral Frieda. There is a Joseph Conrad novel titled *Freya of the Seven Isles*.

Frostine

French

Frostine, best known in the U.S. as the name of the Candyland queen, is newly fashionable in France and is certainly a choice that any little girl the world over would love. Fanciful, if over-the-top.

G

Gardener

Latin, "keeper of the garden"

One of the most pleasant and evocative of the hot new occupational names. Related name: Gardner, as in Ava.

Gardenia

Flower name

More exotic and powerful than garden varieties like Rose and Lily. Named for a botanist appropriately surnamed Garden.

Garland

Word name

Garland is fragrant and celebratory, and also has a celebrity-tribute tie to the star of *The Wizard of Oz*.

Gaynor

Welsh, "white and smooth, soft"

Gaynor is an early androgynous name with a positive association, related to the Cornish megahit name Jennifer.

Gelsey

Persian, "flower"

This name was given a lithe and graceful image by ballerina Gelsey Kirkland, but was later far surpassed by Kelsey and Chelsea.

Ghislaine

gees-LANE

French from German, "pledge"

Ghislaine still sounds exotic to us, even though in France this name — which can be pronounced with a hard or soft initial G — is dated. It can also be spelled Ghislain.

Giulia

JOO-lee-ah

Italian variation of Julia, "youthful"

An Italian version of an English classic beginning to be adopted by cutting-edge American parents, including *Entourage*'s Debi Mazar.

Glory

Word name

Glory sounds fresh and uplifting and a lot more modern than Gloria (which is definitely feeling the stirrings of a revival, though some might still view it as a terminal Old Lady name). Glory, as in "Glory Be" and "Old Glory," has both a religious and a patriotic flavor.

Grania

Irish, variation of Grainne (gran-ya), "the loved one" or "grain of corn"

In addition to being the appellation of an ancient grain goddess, this name was also borne by two mythic Irish figures, one of whom was betrothed to legendary chieftain Finn MacCool, the other the brave sixteenth century pirate Grainne Ni Mhaille — known in English as Grace O'Malley — whose name passed into poetry as a symbol of Ireland. Grania is popular in Ireland and possible here, especially in this Anglicized spelling.

Gray

Color name

This color name, spelled either Gray or Grey is rapidly catching on. Actress Jenny von Oy recently called her daughter Gray Audrey.

Greer

Scottish, contraction of surname Gregor; Latin, "alert, watchful"

Early and still attractive surname choice, popularized by forties Academy Award winner Greer Garson (born Eileen; Greer was her mother's maiden name), and chosen much more recently by Kelsey Grammer for his daughter and by Brooke Shields in the Grier form.

Guinevere

Welsh, "white shadow, white wave"

Guinevere was the name of the ill-fated queen of Camelot, for so many years eclipsed by its modern Cornish form Jennifer. Today, Guinevere could be a cool possibility for adventurous parents intrigued by this richly evocative and romantic choice. Cousin ideas: Gwendolen, Gwyneth, Genevieve, Jenna, or Gwen.

Guthrie

Scottish, "windy spot"

Guthrie, folk singer Woody's last name, makes a perfectly fine first choice for a girl.

Gwendolen

Welsh, "white circle"

A name retired years ago in favor of the short form Gwen, but now, like many other old-fashioned names, this ancient Welsh favorite is up for reappraisal.

Gwendolen is the name of principal characters in George Eliot's novel *Daniel Deronda* and in the Oscar Wilde play, *The Importance of Being Earnest*.

Gypsy

English, "wanderer"

Gypsy, long associated with the intellectual stripper Gypsy Rose Lee and the musical that was made about her life, has a certain exotic charm. Drea de Matteo and Shooter Jennings used it as the middle name of their daughter Alabama.

H

Haidee

English, "modest"

It sounds like a variant of Heidi or Hailey, but Haidee is actually a separate name with a literary history, used in Byron's epic poem *Don Juan*.

Heloise

French from German, "healthy; wide"

Heloise is an ancient name with an uncertain derivation. Is it related to Louise or not? Is Eloise a variation of it or vice versa? Most familiar to Americans as the author of *Household Hints*, Heloise is ready to reclaim its fashion status.

In the twelfth century, the name was borne by the beloved of the French philosopher Pierre Abelard, who was considered to be one of the most learned women of the Middle Ages.

Hermione

her-MY-o-nee

Greek, "messenger, earthly"; feminine variation of Hermes, the Greek messenger god

Hermione's co-starring role in *Harry Potter* has made this previously ignored, stodgy name of the daughter of Venus and Mars, suddenly viable. Hermione could really take off once today's children start having kids of their own.

Hero

Greek mythology name, English word name

Despite the possibility of gender confusion, the Hero in Greek myth was a woman. Myleene Klass got that when she chose Hero for her daughter.

In Greek legend young Leander swam across dangerous waters every night to court his beloved Hero. In Shakespeare's *Much Ado ABout Nothing*, Hero is the love interest of Claudio and cousin of Beatrice.

Holiday

Word name

Free and fun name if you don't want to be pinned down to Noelle, Pasqua, or Valentine.

Holland

Dutch, place-name

One of the coolest geographical names, unadorned and elegant, evocative of fine Rembrandt portraits and fields of pink and yellow tulips.

Honor

Virtue name

Honor is a somewhat more pressured virtue name than Hope or Grace, placing a high standard on any girl carrying it, but it's a goal worth setting. By choosing Honor for her daughter, Jessica Alba brought it very much into the modern world. The more feminine Honora is also pretty and a fresh route to Nora.

Probably the best known bearer is British actress Honor Blackman, remembered for her roles in *The Avengers* and the James Bond *Goldfinger*.

Honoria

Latin, "woman of honor"

This is an eighteenth century elaboration of Honor found in Charles Dickens (*Bleak House*) but rarely heard here and now.

Hyacinth

Flower name

Not as lovely as Lily or as gentle as Jasmine, Hyacinth still might hold some appeal for parents seeking a truly exotic flower name. There was actually a Saint Hyacinth — he (yes, he) was martyred for cutting down a tree used in pagan worship.

I

Ianthe

ee-AN-the

Greek, "purple flower"

Ianthe is the unusual, romantic, almost ethereal Greek name of the mythological daughter of Oceanus, supreme ruler of the sea. It was chosen by the poet Shelley for his daughter.

Ilaria

Italian variation of Hilary, "cheerful, happy"

Hilary is now too connected to a single personality, but this version offers a fresh and interesting alternative.

Imogen

IM-eh-jen

Greek, "beloved child"

Imogen is a Shakespearean name long fashionable in England, which lost its way here when spelled and pronounced im-oh-GENE. Pronounced the British way, Imogen is as pretty and classy as it is distinctive. Imogen also gained attention through its link to Grammy-winning musician Imogen Heap.

Though never in the American Top 1000, Imogen has gained a lot of favor in recent years among stylish parents, so you may find more little Imogens in your hip neighborhood than that statistic would suggest.

On the plus side, Imogen has the wonderful namesake photographer Imogen Cunningham and also a meaning that can't be topped.

Indigo

Color name

Indigo is one of the most appealing and evocative of the new generation of color names. Color names have joined flower and jewel names — in a big way — and

Indigo, a deep blue-purple dye from plants native to India, is particularly striking for both girls and boys. Indigo is the name of a character in the Ntozake Shange novel *Sassafrass, Cypress & Indigo*, and was used for his daughter by Lou Diamond Phillips.

Indira

Sanskrit, "beauty"

Indira might have a more modern, exotic feel were it not for the somewhat middle-aged image of longtime Indian prime minister Indira Gandhi.

Indra

Sanskrit, "possessing drops of rain"

In the ancient Hindu religion, Indra is the warrior god of sky and rain, though in modern America, this might make a better girls' than boys' name. You can spell it Indre, like the French river, if you prefer.

Iolanthe

yo-lan-thuh

Greek, "violet flower"

Iolanthe is known through the Gilbert & Sullivan operetta of that name. Iolanthe is a softer version of Yolanda, but if you find it a bit too weighty, you could try the more stylish English version Violet.

Irina

Russian from Greek, "peace"

Irina is a Russian ballet-inflected classic, one of the Three Sisters in the Chekhov play. If you want to pronounce Irene with three syllables, you might want to clarify things with Irina.

Isabeau

French variation of Isabel, "pledged to God"

With Isabel getting so popular, parents are searching for new varieties of the name, and Isabeau is one that makes a lovely French twist.

Isabeau of Bavaria was the wife of King Charles VI of France. It is also the name of an opera by Pietro Mascagni, a retelling of the medieval English legend of Lady Godiva, and in the 1985 film *Ladyhawke*, Michelle Pfeiffer plays the heroine, Lady Isabeau.

Isabetta

Short form of Elisabetta, Italian variation of Elizabeth, "pledged to God"

Isabetta is a charming spin on both the Elizabeth and Isabella families and a new way to go if you love the originals but want something more, well, original.

Isolde

Welsh, "fair lady"; German "ice ruler"

Now that Tristan has been rediscovered, maybe it's time for his fabled lover in the Arthurian romances and Wagnerian opera, a beautiful Irish princess, to be brought back into the light as well.

This would make an artistic and romantic choice, as the medieval heroine is seen as a symbol of undying — if unhappy — love.

Variations include Iseult, Isolt, Isoud, Isolda and Yseult.

J

Jacinta

hah-SEEN-tah

Spanish for Greek flower name, "hyacinth"

Jacinta, the Spanish word for hyacinth, is a lot softer and sweeter than the English version. Although the name is slightly different, Jacinta is largely associated at present with Australian-born actress Jacinda Barrett.

Jamaica

Place-name

Among the least gimmicky, most appealing and colorful of all the names found in the atlas, Jamaica almost sings out the exotic rhythms of the West Indies. Namesake: writer Jamaica (born Elaine) Kincaid.

Jameson

English, "son of James"

Stylish surname way to go if you want to name a girl after a James, and is more substantial than the passé Jamie; it was chosen for their daughter by Chynna Phillips and Billy Baldwin.

Jenica

Romanian variation of Jane, "God's gracious gift"

Jenica might work if you can't decide between Jennifer and Jessica. It's certainly a more distinctive option.

Jessamine

JEH-sah-meen

Earlier spelling of flower name Jasmine

Jessamine, a charming name occasionally heard in England, is just beginning to be appreciated in the US as a possible successor to all the Jess names of the past. It's also spelled Jessamyn, as in Quaker novelist Jessamyn West, author of *Friendly Persuasion* — who started life with Jessamyn as her middle name.

Jezebel

Hebrew, "pure, virginal"

Jezebel, the wife of King Ahab in the Hebrew Book of Kings, has long had a bad girl reputation. But in the modern secular world, this is somewhat mitigated by the feminist perspective of her as a strong woman, the power behind the throne. Previously avoided as a baby name, Jezebel is now, along with the also previously avoided Delilah and Desiree, coming into use, helped by its relation to other 'bel' name such as Isabel and Bella.

The popular feminist celebrity blog Jezebel upped the name's cool factor.

Jordana

Hebrew, "flowing down"

A feminization used more before Jordan joined the girls' camp.

Jubilee

Hebrew, "ram's horn"

Jubilee has a joyous and jubilant aura, but it wouldn't be an easy name to carry, what with all that pressure to be a living, breathing, 24-7 party. Jubilee was the name selected by television's Duggars for their miscarried child.

Jude

Diminutive of Judith, Hebrew, "He will be praised, or, "Woman from Judea"

Jude may be a rising boys' name but it's also a new way to spin Judy or Judith. Alexis Stewart, daughter of Martha, named her daughter Jude and Jessica Lange plays Sister Jude on *American Horror Story*.

Jules

Latin; Greek, "youthful; soft, downy"

TV personality Jules Asner made this middle-aged male name suddenly seem young and fresh and female, after having been an off-the radar-nickname for Julia and Julie. Author and wife of celebrity chef Jamie Oliver spells her name Jools, and we've also seen Joolz.

Juna

Variation of June, month name

Juna, a variation of the newly stylish month name June, was introduced in the U.S. by actor Bradford Anderson, who chose it for his daughter, whose middle name, Meredith, is the name of Anderson's New Hampshire hometown. Juna may also be thought of as a relative of Djuna, the self-created name of writer Djuna Barnes.

Juno

Latin, "queen of the heavens"

Juno is an ancient name that feels as fresh as if it had been minted — well, not yesterday, but in 2007. Since the release of the popular indie film *Juno,* this lively but strong o-ending Roman goddess name has become more and more prominent as a potential baby name — Coldplay's Will Champion chose Juno for one of his twins (whose brother is the kingly Rex).

Juno was the sister and wife (hmmm) of Jupiter, and the mother of Mars and Vulcan. The patron goddess of Rome and protector of women and marriage, Juno's name is heard in Virgil's *Aeneid*, Shakespeare's *The Tempest*, and Sean O'Casey's play *Juno and the Paycock.*

K

Kalila

Arabic, "beloved"

The lilting name of a range of mythical mountains, with an extensive menu of spellings, and a more unusual way of fitting in with current favorites Lila and Lola.

Kalindi

Hindi, variation of Kalinda, "sun"

Kalindi is a lovely, rhythmic name that refers to one of the seven sacred rivers of India.

Kasiani

Greek, "cinnamon"

Kasiani, also spelled Kassiani or Cassiane, is an ancient Greek name best known as the name of a saint famous as a hymnographer. The Hymn of Kasiani, traditionally sung on Tuesday of Easter Week in the Greek Orthodox Church, is associated with fallen women. The 9th century saint Kasiani was supposed to be in love with the Emperor Theophilos, who rejected her when she proved to be more intelligent than he.

Kat

Diminutive for Katherine, Greek, "pure"

We're hearing Kat more and more being used by Katherines who are tired of Kathy, Kate and Katie. Katti or Kattie is another possibility.

Katya

Russian, diminutive of Ekatarina, Russian variation of Katherine, "pure"

One of the warm and earthy Russian nickname names now coming into style. Denzel Washington gave his daughter the Katia spelling.

Keaton

English place and surname, "shed town"

Keaton is an engaging surname name that's on the rise for both girls and boys. Some parents may use it to honor silent film star Buster Keaton or related to Diane Keaton, but others may see it as a stylish name in keeping with the Kardashian-influenced two-syllable n-ending surname names. Choices similar to Keaton include Keegan and Keenan.

Kelilah

keh-LEE-lah

Hebrew, "crown, laurel"

Kelilah, also spelled Kelila, is a lovely and unusual name that would make a perfect substitute for the trendy Delilah.

Kerala

Indian place-name

Kerala, the name of the most beautiful and touristed state of India, has recently debuted on the U.S. extended popularity list as a first name for girls. And why not? Kerala sounds lovely and rhythmic and in tune with the Kardashian-influenced taste for all names K.

Keren

Hebrew, "strength, power, ram's horn"

Israeli-born singer Keren Ann introduced this traditional Hebrew name to this country, where it could well be mistaken for Karen.

Kerensa

Cornish, "love"

Kerensa, forever exotic, is a romantic Cornish name spelled with an 's' or 'z', the most modern of the Karen family. Kerensa (or Kerenza) has ties to the Welsh Cerys.

Keturah

Hebrew, "incense"

Keturah, the Old Testament name of Abraham's second wife, is a possibility for anyone seeking a truly unusual and interesting biblical name; certainly a lot more distinctive than that of Abraham's first wife, Sarah.

Keturah bore Abraham six sons, who were characterized by one historian as "men of courage and of sagacious minds." Through them, Keturah was the ancestor of sixteen tribes. In the eighteenth century it was believed by some that Keturah was the ancestor of African peoples.

This is a name not readily found in popular culture, though there was a character named Keturah on the TV sci-fi show *Stargate Atlantis* — but he just happened to be male.

Keziah

KEE-zee-ah or KEE-szhah

Hebrew, "cassia tree"

Keziah, also spelled Kezia, is an Old Testament name — she was one of the three daughters of Job — widely used for slaves and still most common in the African-American community. The lovely, distinctive Keziah — along with others like Jemima — deserves full emancipation. Modern parents are also rediscovering the related Cassia. Other variations of Keziah include Kazia, Kaziah, Kessie, Ketzi, Ketzia, Ketziah, Kezia, Kezzie, Kissie, Kizzie, and Kizzy.

Kilala

Sanskrit, "ambrosia"

Kilala is a rhythmic, lilting name that has emerged from the romance and adventure manga series, Kilala Princess. Its double 'l's are very much in synch with others such as Lila, Lola, Lilac, et al.

Kiri

Maori, "tree bark"

The name Kiri was made famous by New Zealand soprano Kiri Te Kanawa, whose original name was Claire. Cute but slight, Kiri is close to several other names from Kiriah to Keira to Kyra and its diminutive Kyrie.

Kirrily

Maori or Aboriginal, "tree bark or leaf"

Kirrily, which rhymes with cheerily, is a name that's uniquely popular in Australia. It originated in recent decades as an elaboration of several similar names — the European Kyra or Keira, the Maori Kiri which means tree bark, or the Aboriginal word kira which means leaf — plus the lee sound. Australian fashion designer Kirrily Johnston has helped popularize the name, which has spawned a countless number of spelling variations.

Kit

English, diminutive of Katherine, "pure"
Kit is a crisp, old-time British-accented nickname that sounds fresh and modern today. Kitty is another so-retro-it's-cool nickname.

Krizia

Italian, diminutive of Lucrezia, Roman family name
Krizia is a stylish Italian clothing and handbag designer and manufacturer. The name is an interesting alternative to all those old Cris/Kris-starting names.

L

Lake

Nature name

This body of water runs deep; the best of a group of new possibilities that includes Bay, Ocean, River, and the more established Brook. It has received attention via the actress Lake Bell.

Lalia

Latin, "speaking well"

A completely undiscovered double-l name with an abundance of rhythmic charm.

Lally

Diminutive of any La- name

A likable nickname-name in the Callie, Hallie mode.

Lane

English, "a small roadway or path"

A unisex name equally accessible to boys and girls. As a common surname, Lane is attached to such celebrities as Diane and Nathan.

Lark

English bird name

Lark is getting some new and well-deserved attention as a post-Robin and Raven bird name. Although it was first recorded as a name in the 1830's, it has never appeared on the Social Security list.

'The Lark' was used as a nickname for Cosette in *Les Miserables*; Lark Voorhees was a star of *Saved by the Bell*, and Jennifer Connelly and Paul Bethany used Lark as the middle name of their daughter Agnes.

The expression "happy as a lark" gives this songbird name a cheery image.

Larkin

Irish, "rough, fierce"

While Larkin takes this name from girlish bird to boyish surname, there are actually more female Larkins these days than male, and it's a name that works as well for either gender.

Lavender

English plant and color name

Lavender lags far behind other sweet-smelling purple-hued Violet and Lilac, but is starting to get some enthusiastic attention from cutting-edge namers. It does have a history as a name, going back to the eighteenth century, when it was also used for boys. Lavender Brown is a *Harry Potter* character.

Lawrence

Latin, "from Laurentium"

We approve of this name for a girl — but prefer the au, Laura-Laurenish, spelling.

Leaf

Nature name

Leaf is a hippieish choice that, for girls, still retains an evergreen quality.

Leith

Scottish, river name

Traditionally a male name, Leith now can make a highly unusual, strong but soft, and intriguing girls' possibility.

Lilac

English, from Persian, flower and color name

Could Lilac be the next Lila or Lily or Violet? It certainly has a lot going for it — those lilting double 'l's, the fabulous fragrance it exudes, and the fact that it's a color name as well, providing a readymade nursery theme.

Actor Stephen Moyer was ahead of the curve when he named his daughter Lilac in 2002.

Lilo

LEE-lo

German, diminutive of Liselotte; Hawaiian, "generous one"

Lilo is the name of the spunky little Hawaiian girl character in the Disney movie *Lilo & Stitch* — and is also Lindsay Lohan's nickname. Multi-cultural, it can be found in Hawaiian, German and Hebrew nomenclature.

Lilou

Occitan pet form of French Liliane, "lily"

Occitan is a language spoken in Provence, in the south of France, in which the suffix "ou" denotes a pet form — thus, Lilou as a short form of Liliane or its Occitan form Liliana or Liliano. Its popularity in France can be traced to the 1997 film *The Fifth Element*. Pronouced lee-loo, this is an enchanting option.

Linden

Tree name

Though this name of a sturdy tree that can live for centuries was quite popular for boys in the first half of the twentieth century, at this point in time we can see Linden as a fresh-sounding possibility for a little girl named to honor an Aunt Linda.

Lotus

Greek, "lotus flower"

One of the most exotic and languorous of the flower names, with intriguing significance in both Buddhism and Hinduism, symbolizing purity, grace and spiritual growth. Lotus Flower is a Chinese character in the 1931 Pulitzer Prize-winning Pearl S. Buck novel, *The Good Earth*.

Lucasta

English, "pure light"

Lucasta was invented by seventeenth century poet Richard Lovelace for a collection of poems dedicated to a lover named Lucy, and is familiar through the Eugene O'Neill play and film *Anna Lucasta*. Lucasta is a distinctive, rarely used choice and a logical extension of the Luke/Luc/Luca names.

Lucienne

loo-SYEN

French, feminine variation of Lucien, "light"

A soft and ultra-sophisticated French-accented option in the Lucy family.

Ludovica

Italian, feminine variation of Ludovic, "famous in war"

Olde World name with a measure of European style — an offbeat possibility for the bold baby namer.

Lux

Latin, "light"

This name of a character played by Kirsten Dunst in the movie *Virgin Suicides*, originally a novel by Jeffrey Eugenides, is gaining attention, also thanks to the heroine Lux, Lady of Luminosity in the *League of Legends* games. Luz is the Spanish version.

Lyle

Scottish and English from French, "someone who lives on an island"

Lyle is a perfect example of a name that sounds old-fashioned for a boy, cool for a girl.

Lyra

Greek, "lyre"

Lyra is a constellation name taken from the lyre of Orpheus. It contains the star Vega and thus could make a melodic choice for a parent interested in music, astronomy, or mythology.

Lyra was chosen for their daughter by Sophie Dahl and Jamie Cullum. Lyra Belacqua is the heroine of Philip Pullman's *Golden Compass* series.

M

Madigan

Irish, "little dog"

An unusual, energetic surname choice that would make a good Madison alternative. *Madigan* was a typical police detective series of the 1970s, starring Richard Widmark.

Magee

ma-GEE

Irish, "son of Hugh"

Magee became one of the first gender-bending Irish surname names so popular today thanks to New York television newswoman Magee Hickey. In case you don't know, the g is hard, as in Maggie, but with the opposite emphasis.

Mairead

Irish, shortened form of Mairghread, variation of Margaret, "pearl"

Pronounced MAW-rayt or ma-REYD, Mairead is close enough to Maureen to be accepted here. The name became popular in Ireland due to admiration for the saint of that name. Peig and Peigi are its Irish-language nicknames.

Mairi

Scottish variation of Mary, "bitter"

Why does Mairi, pronounced MAW-re, seem so much cooler than Mary? This Irish form of Mary was not used before the seventeenth century, as it was considered too sacred. Some of its Anglicized forms include Moira, Maura and Maurya.

Maisie

Scottish diminutive of Margaret, "pearl"

Maisie, a hundred-year-old favorite, is in perfect tune with today. Spelled Maisy in a popular children's book series, Maisie is rising in tandem with cousin Daisy. While Maisie might be short for Margaret, Mary, or even a name like Melissa or Marissa, it stands perfectly well on its own.

In literature, Maisie is the name of the precocious young title character in the Henry James novel *What Maisie Knew*, and is also the main female character in Rudyard Kipling's *The Light That Failed*. And to bring things up to date, Maisie is a half-blood character in the *Harry Potter* series.

Malika

Arabic, "queen"; Swahili, "angel"; feminine of Malik, "master"
Malika is an attractive multi-cultural name — it is also a pet form of Amalia in Hungary.

Malika Haqq is an actress who is one of Khloe Kardashian's BFFs on *Keeping Up With the Kardashians*.

Malou

Combination of Mary and Lou, "bitter; renowned warrior"
This charming name, popular in France and the Netherlands, has not traveled to the U.S. yet but would make a modern way to honor grandma Mary or Louise, or as a perfect short form of Mary Louise. Or, with the growing fashion for nickname names, it can stand perfect well on its own. One of several similar variations — Lou, Lilou, Louane — in vogue in Europe.

Manet

man-AY

French artist name
Manet is the accessible, attractive name of an Impressionist great; it could be the next Monet.

Manon

French, diminutive of Marie, "bitter"
Manon is well used in France; it has the exotic yet straightforward feel that makes it a viable import. *Manon of the Spring* was a gorgeous French film. British actors Damian Lewis, of *Homeland*, and Helen McCrory have a daughter named Manon.

Maple

Tree name

If Apple and Juniper, Oak and Pine can be baby names, why not Maple? Why not indeed. We've heard Maple starting to be used quietly, but with its lush sound and attractive image, we predict its use as a first name will grow — and its recent choice by the Jason Batemans — who combined it with the sweet middle name Sylvie — will only accelerate that growth.

Marbella

Spanish place name

The name of the resort city on Spain's Costa del Sol is pronounced mar-BAY-a, setting it apart from the bella-name competition.

March

Word name

March has never been popular as a month name, possibly because of its brisk, masculine beat. But with all kinds of month — and season, day, and holiday — names, from January to December, Sunday to Easter, Winter to Midnight, coming to the fore, March is beginning to seem eminently baby-ready.

Marcheline

French, "warrior"

Marcheline was the first name of Angelina Jolie's late mother, who was part French-Canadian, which Jolie and Brad Pitt used as the middle name for their twin daughter Vivienne. The name is related to the Latin Marcellus and Marcus, which come from Mars, the name of the God of War, and is often spelled Marceline. Jolie's mother's birth name was Marcia Lynne.

Margit

German, Scandinavian and Hungarian diminutive of Margaret, "pearl"

One of the dozens of international variations of Margaret, this one sounds a lot like the original. Marit is another Scandinavian version.

Marielle

Dutch and French diminutive of Mary, "bitter"

Mariel Hemingway made us aware of the more abbreviated spelling of this charming name, which dates back to the nineteenth century.

Marigold

Flower name

Marigold, once found almost exclusively in English novels and aristocratic nurseries, is beginning to be talked about and considered here; it does have a sunny, golden feel. The marigold was the symbol of the Virgin Mary.

Marine

Latin, "from the sea"

Marine is an extremely popular and fashionable name in France that's virtually unknown here — and is ready to set sail. Marine feels more contemporary than Marina and less hippie-esque than Oceane, another popular name for girls in France.

Mariposa

Spanish, "butterfly"

Mariposa is a rare, romantic choice with an intriguing meaning.

Maris

Latin, "of the sea"

Maris is an unusual and appealing name that has never appeared in the US Top 1000, overshadowed by its twentieth century elaboration, Marisa/Marissa. It derives from the phrase "Stella Maris," star of the sea, one of the many epithets of the Virgin Mary, and became familiar via the unseen(but unliked) character of sitcom Frasier's ex-sister-in-law.

As a surname, Maris is associated with legendary NY Yankee, Roger Maris.

Marit

Aramaic, "lady"; Norwegian and Swedish variation of Margaret, "pearl"

An unusual and straightforward name with an attractive Scandinavian accent; a royal name in Norway.

Marlowe

Variation of Marlow, English, "driftwood"

Is it Marlo, Marlow, or Marlowe? When you know the spelling, the 'w' makes a big difference between swinging modern girl name and buttoned-up surname.

Jason Schwartzman used this version for his young daughter, Marlowe Rivers, as did Sienna Miller for her baby girl Marlowe Ottoline. While we love the *o*-sound at the end and think that Marlo or Marlow or Marlowe, however it's spelling, has an attractively lush sound, we'd call this surname variation a bit confusing.

Mattea

ma-TAY-a

Italian, from Hebrew, "gift of God"

This pretty, exotic feminization of Matthew was chosen by Mira Sorvino for her daughter, Mattea Angel.

Mauve

French, "violet-colored"

Mauve is an offbeat color name whose soft and sentimental Victorian spirit is conveyed by the name. One of the newer color names like Blue, Gray and Plum — that are increasingly being used as novel middle names.

Mazarine

French color name

Mazarine is a deep blue color also used as a first name in honor of Cardinal Mazarin, a leader of France in the 17th century. As a first name, Mazarine is as charming as it is unusual.

Melania

Spanish and Greek variation of Melanie, "black"

The current Mrs. Donald Trump, Slovenian model Melania Knauss, brought this pretty version to the fore. Saint Melania was an heiress who freed thousands of slaves.

Melia

Greek mythology nymph, also diminutive of Amelia, "work"

This is a rich, melodic shortening of the British Number 1 Amelia that can stand on its own.

Melisande

French form of Millicent, "strong, industrious"

This old-time fairy tale name is rarely heard in the modern English-speaking world, but it's so, well, mellifluous, that it would make a lovely choice for a twenty-first century girl.

Pelleas and Melisande is a play by Maeterlinck, the inspiration for the Debussy opera of the same name. In modern times, Melisande became a princess via the Rankin and Bass film *The Flight of Dragons*.

Merida

Latin, "one who has achieved a high place of honor"

You'll probably be hearing more of this name thanks to the newest Pixar film, featuring Princess Merida, the first Pixar princess — a feisty, athletic, independent medieval Scottish girl with wild red hair. Her name, however, is not Scottish, but a Spanish place name found in both Spain and Mexico's Yucatan peninsula.

Will Merida be the next Ariel? Stay tuned.

Merritt

English surname, "boundary gate"

This unusual unisex surname name is heard more often on girls these days than it was (way) back in the day.

Merritt was a female character in the 1980s flick *Where the Boys Are*, and Merritt Wever plays the endearingly awkward young Nurse Zoey on *Nurse Jackie*.

Mirabel

Latin, "wonderful"

Mirabel is one of those names that's not on the Top 1000 but ought to be — and undoubtedly will be soon. There's a real resurgence of 'bel' names like Isabel and Annabel, and Mirabel, a more unusual and elegant example, which has a wonderful Latin meaning, is also the name of a delicate French plum spelled Mirabelle.

Mirabel and the Italian form Mirabella were both quite common in the later Middle Ages, and Mirabel is scattered throughout early English poetry.

Mirabel has a nice pair of nickname options — Mira and Belle.

Mirren

Irish, meaning unknown

Mirren is one modern spelling of a mysterious group of names that all seem to derive from the sixth century Irish saint Mirin who emigrated to Scotland and now is the patron saint of both the Glasgow suburb of Paisley and the game of football. The Cornish Merryn, best known as the name of the seacoast town St. Merryn, is also related. The name is usually used for girls.

Morning

Word name

There are many lovely day/month/seasonal names — and this is one of the most intriguing.

Murphy

Irish, "hound of the sea"

This surname name popularized for girls by TV's *Murphy Brown* back in the 80's and 90's still has some breezy energy.

N

Navy

Word name

When R & B singer Nivea made this highly original choice for her daughter's name, she claimed to have thought of it in terms of the color and not the seagoing armed service. You can look at it either way.

Nerissa

Greek, "from the sea"

An offbeat possible replacement for the overused Melissa and Marisa, Nerissa was used by Shakespeare for Portia's witty confidante in *The Merchant of Venice*. Queen Elizabeth hasa cousin named Nerissa.

Neve

neev

Latin, "snow"; Anglicized spelling of Niamh, "bright"

Introduced to the American public by actress Neve Campbell — it was her Dutch-born mother's maiden name — Neve is an interesting and fresh new possibility, one which Conan O'Brien chose for his daughter.

Niamh

neev

Irish Gaelic, "bright"

Niamh is an ancient Irish name that was originally a term for a goddess; rich in legendary associations. In Irish myth, one who bore it was Niamh of the Golden Hair, daughter of the sea god, who fell in love with Finn's son Oisin/Ossian and takes him to the Land of Promise, where they stayed three hundred years.

Niamh is in the Irish Top 25, and is also well used in England and Scotland. Here, the phonetic Neve (see above) would undoubtedly prove simpler, if less intriguing.

Nica

Short form of Veronica, Latin, "true image"

More often spelling Nika, this is a well-used diminutive for the Eastern European Veronika, and there's no reason that the same principle can't apply in the West. It makes a venerated saint's name sound fresh and cute.

Noa

Hebrew, "movement, motion"

This Old Testament female name has been the most popular girls' name in Israel over the last decade. Also in the Top 100 in Spain, it will probably be misunderstood here as an attempt to streamline and feminize the more familiar Noah.

Noor

Hindi, "light"

An interesting name associated with the elegant American-born Queen Noor of Jordan. Noor is very popular among modern Muslim parents around the world and is beginning to cross over, perhaps because of its simplicity and its resemblance to the stylish Western Nora.

Norris

French, "northerner"

A British surname that was used only for males until Mrs. Norman Mailer, Norris Church (born Barbara), came under the public eye.

November

Latin, "ninth month"

The menu of usable month names seems to expand every, well, month, with such choices as November, October, and January joining more established names like April, May, June and August. Most are more appropriate for girls, with logical November nicknames such as Nova, Novi, or Ember sounding particularly feminine.

Nuala

NOO-la

Irish, short form of Fionnuala, "white shoulders"

Officially a shortening of the traditional and tricky Gaelic Fionnghuala/ Fionnuala, Nuala makes a lovely choice all on its own.

O

Oakley

English, "oak wood or clearing"

The Annie Oakley connection makes this a bit more girl-appropriate.

Oceane

French, "ocean"

This is a wildly popular name in France that could easily cross the ocean, and is much more stylish than the English Ocean.

October

Word name

So much more memorable and modern than April or May, October was chosen by innovative author/editor Dave Eggers for his daughter.

Oona

Irish, variation of Una, "lamb:

Oona is a name made famous by Eugene O'Neill's daughter, who became Charlie Chaplin's wife; the double-*o* beginning gives it a lot of oomph.

In Irish legend, Una/Ona was a daughter of a king of Lochlainn. The name was very popular in Ireland in the Middle Ages, and is currently seeing a comeback — also spelled Oonagh.

Orchid

Flower name

This is an exotic hothouse bloom that has not been plucked by many modern baby namers — yet. In the language of flowers, orchids symbolize love, beauty and sophistication. In a 1926 silent comedy, femme fatale Gloria Swanson played a burlesque chorus girl named Orchid Murphy.

Oriana

Latin, "dawn"

Oriana is a dashing medieval name, with a meaning similar to Aurora. Strong and exotic, Oriana also has an admirable literary resume. In medieval tales, she was the beloved of the knight Amadis, she appears in at least three seventeenth century plays, and there is an early Tennyson poem called *The Ballad of Oriana*. Oriana was also sometimes used to refer to Queen Elizabeth I.

Ottavia

Italian, variation of Latin Octavia, "eight"

Softer and more exotic than Octavia, this is a name once used when it wasn't uncommon for families to have eight children. A possible substitute for the epidemically popular Olivia.

Ottoline

French and English, diminutive of Odile, "prospers in battle"

Curiously appealing, in a hoop-skirted, wasp-waisted way, Ottoline has recently entered the realm of modern possibility, especially since Sienna Miller chose it as the middle name of her daughter Marlowe.

Lady Ottoline Morrell was an influential British aristocrat who was a force in the artistic and literary community of her day.

Ovidia

Feminine variation of Ovidius, Roman family name, "shepherd or sheep"

Ovidia is the unusual feminine form of the ancient Roman Ovidius, most famous as the name of the exiled 1st century Roman poet Ovid. Modern male form Ovidio is known in Spain and Portugal. Ovida is another variation.

P

Pallas

Greek, "wisdom"

This rarified Greek name — in classical mythology Pallas Athena was the goddess of wisdom and the arts — might appeal to literary-minded parents.

Paz

pahz

Hebrew, "golden"; Spanish, "peace"

Paz, currently represented by actress Paz Vega, would make a sparkling middle name choice. It originated as a title of the Virgin Mary — Our Lady of Peace.

Peony

Flower name; Latin, "healing"

One of the rarest of the floral names, though not without some teasing potential. *Peony* is a historical 1948 novel by Pearl S. Buck.

Perdita

Latin, "lost"

A Shakespearean invention for an abandoned baby in *The Winter's Tale*, PErdita's sense of loss has always been off-putting to parents. But her image was somewhat resuscitated by its association with the appealing canine character in Disney's *One Hundred and One Dalmations*.

Peri

Greek; Hebrew; Persian, "mountain dweller; fruit; fairy"

This name used for both sexes in several cultures is quite well used in Israel.

Persephone

per-SEF-o-nee

Greek, "bringing death"

Persephone is the esoteric name of the Greek mythological daughter of Zeus by Demeter, the queen of the harvest. After she was kidnapped by Pluto to be

Queen of the Underworld, it was decreed by Jupiter that she would spend six months of the year with her mother, allowing crops to grow, and six in mourning, thus accounting for the seasons.

Despite the mixed message of her mythological past, Persephone has a light and lyrical aura, and pleasant associations with springtime and the harvest — she was also goddess of Spring. Persephone was seen in the *Matrix* movies, played by Monica Bellucci, and could make an interesting replacement for the overused Stephanie.

Persis

Greek, "Persian woman"

Parents seeking a distinctive New Testament name might consider this one. Adopted by some Puritans in the seventeenth century, Persis was used in the William Dean Howells novel *The Rise of Silas Lapham* for the wife of the protagonist.

Petal

Greek word and flower name

Petal is the soft and sweet-smelling name of a character in the novel and film, *The Shipping News*. With the rise of such flower names as Poppy and Posy, we believe Petal — down-to-earth yet exotic — has its own appealingly distinctive style.

Celebrity chef Jamie Oliver named his daughter Petal Blossom Rainbow in 2009.

Phaedra

FAY-drah

Greek, "bright"

This name of a tragic figure in Greek mythology, the daughter of King Minos, sister of Ariadne and wife of Theseus, has a mysterious and intriguing appeal.

Phaedra has been a persistent theme in literature, both ancient and modern. There have been plaus by Euripedes, Racine, Unamuno, and O'Neill, novels, poetry, operas and film — as recently as the 2011 *Immortals* starring Freida Pinto.

Philippa

Greek, feminine variation of Philip, "lover of horses"

Philippa is a prime example of a boy's name adapted for girls that was common as crumpets in Cornwall, but was as rare as reindeer meat in Miami — until the advent of royal sister-in-law Philippa Middleton, who goes by the lively nickname Pippa.

Philippa has been fashionable in England since the fourteenth century when King Edward married Philippa of Hainault.

Philippine

French, feminine variation of Philippe, "lover of horses"
Philippine would be taken as an ethnic identification rather than a name in the U.S. Better try Philippa, though if you don't mind eternally correcting people, Philippine can make an interesting alternative. Pippa can be a short form of Philippine as well as Philippa.

Pia

Latin, "pious"; diminutive of Olympia, "from Mount Olympus"
Soft name in the Mia-Nia-Tia family, Pia is heard in both European and Hindi languages.

Pilar

Spanish, "pillar"
The nonvowel ending of this Spanish classic, which honors the Virgin Mary, gives it a special sense of strength, elegance, and style, making it a worthy choice. Pilar is remembered as the valiant heroine of Hemingway's *For Whom the Bell Tolls*.

Pippa

English, diminutive of Philippa, "lover of horses"
Pippa, a condensation of Philippa that turns it from serious to sprightly, has come into the public eye in a big way via the former Kate Middleton's sister.

Heard far more in the UK than the US, Pippa has been used on its own since the nineteenth century, popularized by Robert Browning's dramatic poem, *Pippa Passes*. A recent film was titled *The Private Lives of Pippa Lee*.

Pippa can and is given as a name in its own right, and may also be short for names other than Philippa: Penelope, for instance, or Patricia, or the more exotic Philippine.

Pixie

Swedish or Cornish, "fairy"

Pixie is a cute – some might think too cute — name that suddenly feels possible thanks to the craze for names that contain the letter x. Though its origin may be uncertain, a pixie is internationally recognized as a sprite or fairy: tiny, sometimes green, usually pointy-eared.

Placida

Italian and Spanish, "serene"

A name that's more familiar in its male form, Placido, but this can be a similar-feeling alternative to Serena.

Plum

Fruit name

British-born novelist Plum Sykes has taken this fruity name out of the produce section and put it into the baby name basket. It's more appealing than Apple, more presentable than Peaches. The French equivalent, Prune, is very fashionable there but would not fly with English speakers.

Poet

Word name

A recently entered name on the roster, Poet was used for her daughter by Soleil Moon (Punky Brewster) Frye, who obviously appreciates the advantages of an unusual name.

Pomeline

French, related to "apple"

A rarely heard — even in France — name, most prominent as the third name of Charlotte Marie Pomeline Casiraghi, the daughter of Princess Caroline of Monaco and granddaughter of Grace Kelly.

Poppy

Latin flower name

Poppy, unlike most floral names which are sweet and feminine, has a lot of spunk; Poppy makes an especially good choice for a redhead. Jamie Oliver — the British "Naked Chef" — used Poppy for his daughter. Poppy is currently in the UK Top 20.

One notable Poppy is Australian *Without a Trace* star Poppy Montgomery (full name Poppy Petal Emma Elizabeth — her mother named all her daughters after flowers).

Other Poppy-like names to consider: Pippa and Piper and Petal.

Posy

English, "a bunch of flowers"

Posy has been long fashionable in England, a country of gardeners, but this pretty bouquet-of-flowers name is still rarely heard here, though it could be seen as a more unusual possible alternative to Rosy or Josie.

Posy is a little sister name in the *Hunger Games* series. Before that, Posy Fossil was a character in Noel Streatfield's *Ballet Shoes*.

Posy (or Posey) could also work as a nickname for a range of other names, from Penelope to Sophia. Other P-beginning flower names you may want to consider along with Posey: Poppy, Petal, Primrose.

Primrose

English, "first rose"; flower name

Still found in quaint British novels, and until recently considered a bit too prim for most American classrooms, some adventurous namers are suddenly beginning to see Primrose as an attractive member of the rose family. In the 90's British TV series, *The Darling Buds of May*, there is a character named Primrose Violet Anemone Iris Magnolia Narcissa Larkin.

Priya

Sanskrit, "beloved"

A name traditionally given to Indian girls born in August, Priya — pronounced pree-ah — denotes someone with an individual brand of beauty.

Puck

Literary name

Puck, the mischievous sprite of Shakespeare, is a unisex name given more often to girls in The Netherlands and is also the name of one of the moons of Uranus, discovered in 1985 and named Puck for the Shakespearean character.

Q

Quincy

French from Latin, "estate of the fifth son"

Quincy is a Presidential surname name that actually sounds both cute and strong when used for a girl.

R

Rain

Word name

Among a small shower of rain-related names, this pure version can have, depending on how you look at it, a fresh or a gloomy image.

Richard Pryor named his now-grown daughter Rain, and Rain is also one of the nature-named Phoenix family siblings.

Raleigh

English, "meadow of deer"

An attractive North Carolina unisex place name, Raleigh's soft sound is particularly appropriate for a girl.

Raphaela

Hebrew, feminine variation of Raphael, "God has healed"

A euphonious and lovely name with a dark-eyed, long-flowing-haired image, Raphaella is, like Gabriella and Isabella, beginning to be drawn into the American mainstream.

Reeve

English occupational name, "bailiff"

Chosen by aviators Charles and Anne Lindbergh for their daughter, Reeve is another single-syllable surname waiting to be borrowed by the girls.

Remember

Word name

No one will ever forget it. But Remember as a name came over on the Mayflower, so it has deep history as well as modern potential.

Remi

French, variation of Remy, "oarsman"

Adorable name that's fashionably but (still) quietly used. While many parents prefer this spelling for a girl, the Remy version is perfectly appropriate as well.

Reverie

Word name

Reverie is a strong-sounding word for an ethereal, dreamlike state — a perfect contrast and meaning for a word that intends to become a first name. Popular mommy blogger Rebecca Woolf of *Girls Gone Child* named one of her twin daughters Reverie, setting off a groundswell of interest.

Rhonwen

Welsh, "slender, fair"

The delicate and haunting Welsh Rhonwen is still a rarity in the U.S., where her English version Rowena is better known, but would be a lovely choice for any parent in search of a name that was both unusual and traditional, classically feminine yet strong. Related choices to consider: Bronwen, Anwen, and Olwen.

Ripley

English, "strip of clearing in the woods"

The name Ripley reflects the powerful character played by Sigourney Weaver in the *Alien* films; it was chosen by actress Thandie Newton for her daughter.

Róisìn

roh-sheen

Irish diminutive of Rose

Pronounced ro-sheen, this name is very popular in Ireland. Though the Gaelic spelling might lead to some confusion here, the sound is pretty enough to make it worth considering.

Singer Sinead O'Connor has a daughter named Róisìn.

Romilly

English, "man of Rome"

By definition a male name springing from the Roman twin Romulus, this attractive name was introduced to the English-speaking world by painter Augustus John who used it for his son. Romilly John became Admiral of the

Fleet in England. A French surname from the twelfth century on, it's more recently been heard as a girls' name; Emma Thompson used Romilly as her daughter Gaia's middle name.

Romola

Latin, "Roman woman"

Romola is a literary name created by George Eliot for her eponymous 1862 novel set in fifteenth century Florence. It just may appeal to the parent looking for a name that embodies the ideal blend of the feminine, exotic, and strong.

Romy

Diminutive of Rosemary, combination of Rose and Mary; herb name

Actress Romy Schneider seemed to be the singular bearer of this international nickname name until it found new style currency in the past decade. Like other Ro-names — Roman, Rowan, and Romeo — Romy has gained favor with the celebrity set. Matt Lauer has a daughter named Romy, as do director Sofia Coppola and Phoenix frontman Thomas Mars.

Rosamund

German, "horse protection"

A quintessentially British appellation, also spelled Rosamond, this is the name of a legendary twelfth-century beauty. Rare on these shores, it is more than worthy of importation.

Early on, the appellation was associated with 'fair Rosamond,' mistress of Henry II, whose story was the basis of the Joseph Addison opera *Rosamund* and the Swinburne play of the same name. Rosamund Vincy is a character in George Eliot's novel *Middlemarch*.

Rudy

German, short form of Rudolph, "famous wolf"

Rudy hasn't yet enjoyed the comeback of cousin name Ruby, despite having been chosen by hip couple Sadie Frost and Jude Law, but it still could happen.

Rudy has a lot going for it as a usable-on-its-own nickname name, with the lively 'oo' sound found in Jude and Juno and all the popular Lu-starting names. And it was a heartthrob name back in the day when crooner Rudy (born Hubert) Vallee and Rudy/Rudolph (born Rodolpho) Valentino had ladies swooning, reaching as high as Number 299 in 1926.

It has most often been seen as an all-male name — except for little Rudy on *The Cosby Show*.

Rue

English, from Greek, "aromatic medicinal plant"; also word name, "regret"

Rue has gone from *Golden Girls* actress to *Hunger Games* heroine. This botanical name is also a double word name, meaning regret in English and street in French, and has real potential as a middle name.

S

Sacha

French variation of Sasha, diminutive of Alexander, "defending warrior"

Sasha in all its forms — which include Sacha and Sascha — is rising in popularity for both boys and girls, especially with the Sasha spelling attached to one of the First Daughters.

Saffron

Flower and spice name

Spice names are increasingly appealing to the senses of prospective parents; this one has a vaguely orange-scented-incense sixties feel.

English actress Saffron Burrows is an attractive current representative.

Sahar

Arabic, "dawn, morning, awakening"

This is a Muslim name commonly heard in the Middle East.

Sahara

Arabic, "desert"

A beautiful and evocative place-name that deserves wider use.

Sailor

Occupational name

Supermodel Christie Brinkley launched an entire name genre when she picked this breezy occupational name for her daughter n 1998.

Sam

Diminutive of Samantha, "told by God"

Sam is a hot nickname name . . . for girls. Yes, some parents — among them Tiger Woods and Denise Richards and Charlie Sheen — are cutting straight to the simple, unfussy unisex Sam, bypassing the post-trendy Samantha completely.

Samar

Arabic, "evening conversation"

This lovely Arabic name is gaining popularity in the US, used equally for boys and girls. Indeed, its sound (it rhymes with the feminine Tamar but ends with the fashionably masculine -ar sound, as in Oscar) and most logical nickname (Sam) make it a choice that's at once accessible and exotic for both boys and girls.

Sanne

sah-na

Dutch, diminutive of Susanne, "lily"

Sanne is hugely popular in the Netherlands, but almost unknown here — which makes it an interesting prospect for the parent in search of an unusual name. Pronounced sah-na, Sanne is in keeping with the Dutch taste for nicknames plucked from the middle or end of a name vs. the beginning, such as Bas for Sebastien or Bram for Abram.

Saoirse

Irish, "liberty"

Saoirse, a popular name in Ireland used since the 1920s revolution as a statement of freedom, would have some obvious pronunciation problems here. The correct pronunciation is sare-sha. Young Oscar nominee Saoirse Ronan has brought the name into the international public eye, and made it a more plausible choice.

Saskia

Dutch, Saxon, meaning "knife"

Saskia is one of those names that's been used in Europe (she was Rembrandt's wife) since the Middle Ages, but has never crossed the ocean. A charming choice for the adventurous parent, one of whom is TV's Anne Dudek, who chose it for her daughter.

Satine

French, "smooth, shiny"

Satine, the name of the Nicole Kidman character in *Moulin Rouge*, is, by definition satiny smooth. Jacinda Barrett named her daughter Satine Anais.

Savita

Hindi, "sun"

Savita is a popular Indian choice that could easily immigrate. Want some similar ideas? How about the Italian or Spanish Sarita?

Scout

Word name

Scout, a character nickname from *To Kill a Mockingbird* (her real name was Jean Louise) became a real-life possibility when Bruce Willis and Demi Moore used it for their now grown middle daughter, followed by Tom Berenger a few years later. A unisex choice that is growing in popularity for both genders, it was picked by skater Tai Babilonia for her son.

Sela

SEH-lah or SEE-lah

Hebrew, "rock"; also Polynesian variation of Sarah, "princess"

Sela is a Biblical place-name, the original term for the city of Petra, finding new life through actress Sela Ward and also the young daughter of singer Lauryn Hill, who spells it Selah. Found on early African-American slave lists, it was sometimes spelled Cela or Cella.

Senara

Variation of Azenor, Breton, "light"

The origins of Senara, the name of a Cornish saint who is patron of the village of Zennor, are not so straightforward. Some say she was the same person as Azenor, a legendary Breton princess whose mother-in-law cast her out to sea in a trunk. Other stories say she was a mermaid turned Christian. Wherever she came from Senara is that rarest of names: lovely, straightforward, and unusual all at the same time. Since it may be related to Helen or Eleanor, it can be used as an honorific for one of those names — though grandma Helen may understandably think it's a stretch.

Seraphina

Hebrew, "ardent; fiery"

Seraphina is the Number 2 most-searched name on Nameberry, yet is not quite yet in the overall US Top 1000 — though we predict it won't be long before it will be solidly among its ranks. The highest-ranking angels, the six-winged seraphim, inspired the lovely name Seraphina, which was brought into the contemporary spotlight when chosen by high-profile parents Jennifer Garner and Ben Affleck.

Latinate version Serafina is also getting some attention; the name is enjoying a style revival thanks to the current taste for strong, old-fashioned, yet elaborately feminine names. Seraphina has much in common with top choices Isabella, Sophia, and Olivia, and we predict it could be within the US Top 100 in the next decade.

For now, Seraphina remains a beautiful, distinctive choice. Other name ideas if you like Seraphina: Raphaela, Angelica, Serena, and Sabrina.

Seraphine

French from Hebrew, "burning ones"

Seraphine is the Gallic version of the angelic name Seraphina. But while Seraphina has been rising rapidly since Jennifer Garner and Ben Affleck chose it for their second daughter, Seraphine has been largely ignored, though we believe the French vowel-sound ending will soon be more stylish than the *a*-endings that have predominated in girls' names for years.

Another cousin, Seraphita, is the heroine of an eponymous 1837 Balzac novel.

Seren

seh-ren

Welsh, "star"

Seren is a top girls' name in Wales and a lovely choice almost unknown elsewhere. Seren was an ancient goddess of the hot springs.

Severine

French, feminine variation of Severus; Latin, "stern"

This long-popular name in France sounds fresh and unusal here. Severine is the name of the latest James Bond Girl.

Shaw

English, "lives by the thicket"

Shaw is a streamlined and more modern-sounding Shawn, with many notable surname namesakes.

Sheba

Hebrew, short variation of Bathsheba, "daughter of an oath"

This exotic biblical place-name for the region now known as Yemen is given to puppies and kittens more often than babies. But it did start to feel fresh again as the name of the heroine of Zoe Heller's *Notes on a Scandal*, played by on screen by Cate Blanchett.

Shoshana

Hebrew, "lily"

This is an exotic and lovely form of Susannah commonly heard in Israel. Shoshana Shaunbaum is the character played by Zosia Mamet on the hit HBO series *Girls* — a fact that could give the name an upward thrust.

Shula

Hebrew, diminutive of Shulamit, "peace"

Shula is a short form often used on its own in Israel. Sula is another, related, option.

Sidonie

Latin, "from Sidon "

Sidonie is an appealing and chic French favorite that is starting to attract some American fans as a fresher alternative to Sydney. Also spelled Sidony, Sidonie was the birth name of the French novelist Colette.

Signy

Scandinavian, "new victory"

Signy — also spelled Signe — would make another distinctively offbeat alternative to Sydney. Signy appears in Norse mythology as the twin sister of Sigmund.

Sinclair

Scottish, "from the town of St. Clair"

The most famous Sinclair was the (male) writer Lewis, but these days the name works at least as well for a girl.

Sinéad

shin-AID

Irish form of Janet, "God is gracious"

One of the best known of the Irish girls' names, thanks to singer Sinead

O'Connor. It's no longer as fashionable in Ireland as Aoife or Aisling, but by now everyone in the Western World knows it's pronounced shin-aid.

Siobhán

zhuh-VAHN

Irish Gaelic variation of Joan, feminine form of John, "the Lord is gracious"

A lovely Irish name whose perplexing spelling has inspired many phonetic variations, but using the original form preserves the integrity of one of the most beautiful Gaelic girls' names.

The name of several early Irish queens, the name was introduced to the American public by acress Siobhan McKenna. There have been a wide variety of fictional Siobhans, from a Detective Sergeant in the *John Rebus* novels to a vampire in Stephanie Meyers's *Breaking Dawn* to a character in J. K. Rowling's *The Casual Vacancy.*

Snow

Word name

Brisk, fresh, evocative, strange — and magical. A haunting middle name choice.

Solange

SO-LAHNZH

French, "with solemnity"

This is a soignée French name that has never made it here (though it is the name of Beyoncé's less famous sister), but would make a striking, sophisticated choice. Pronunciation: so-LAHNZH.

Soleil

SO-LAY

French, "sun"

An attractive French word name known here via former child TV star Soleil Moon Frye, aka Punky Brewster. It started to be lightly used in the US in the 1920's.

Sonnet

Word name

Could there be a more poetic name than Sonnet? Actor Forest Whitaker chose it for his daughter. Other names beyond Sonnet that can work for the child of a writer or book-lover: Story, Poet, Fable.

Sorcha

SOR-ca

Irish, "bright, shining"

A popular Irish name virtually unknown here — with a pronunciation that's far from obvious. It's basically SOR-ca, but with a little hiccup between the '*r*' and the '*c*' that's near-impossible for the English speaker to reproduce. Other phonetic pronunciations given are sir-eh-ka, sur-aka and surk-ha. Spelled Sorsha, she is a major character in the movie *Willow*.

Sorrel

Botanical name and French, "reddish brown"

A fragrant herbal and color name that could make a sensitive, distinctive choice.

Sparrow

Nature name, "sparrow, a bird"

With related choices such as Lark and Phoenix gaining popularity, why not Sparrow? Though it's usually thought of as a female name, Nicole Richie and Joel Madden chose it for their son.

Spencer

French, "keeper of provisions"

Yes, Spencer makes a plausible and powerful female choice these days, though still thought of as primarily for boys. Kelsey Grammer used it for his daughter in the 1980's.

Story

Word name

An imaginative choice with an uptempo Cory/Rory/Tori sound, perfect for the child of a writer — or anyone with a good story to tell. It has been finding some appreciation among celebs like Minnie Driver and others as a middle name.

Sunniva

SOON-ee-v a

Scandinavian, "sun gift"

Sunniva was an Irish-born saint who fled to Norway, where she hid in an island cave with her followers and eventually died. After miracles were reported on the island, the cave was excavated and Sunniva's intact body was found. Sunniva is the patron saint of Western Norway. Her name would make a fascinating and unusual choice for a modern baby girl, and if her story is a bit grim, you can take refuge in the upbeat nickname Sunny or Sunni.

Suri

Hebrew, variation of Sarah, "princess"

Suri, a once obscure exotic name, hit the headlines when chosen by Katie Holmes and Tom Cruise for their daughter in 2007. Multi-cultural, it also means "the sun" in Sanskrit, "rose" in Persian, and is the name of the Andean Alpaca's wool, as well as a Yiddish form of Sarah, a title used for Jain monks, and a Japanese word for pickpocket.

Suri has not been picked up on by many other parents.

Sylvie

French variation of Latin Sylvia, "from the forest"

Although Sylvia seems to be having somewhat of a revival among trendsetting babynamers, we'd still opt for the even gentler and more unusual Sylvie. Jason Bateman chose it as the middle name of his daughter Maple.

T

Tally

Diminutive of Talia, "gentle dew from heaven"

Nickname sometimes heard on its own, sort of an updated Sally and playmate of Hallie.

Talullah

Irish, Anglicized variation of Tuilelaith, "lady of abundance"; Choctaw, "leaping water"

With memories of the outragrous actress Talullah Bankhead fading, this hauntingly euphonious Choctaw name has re-entered the public domain. A modern hipster favorite, it's been chosen for their daughters by Philip Seymour Hoffman, Patrick Dempsey, Damian Dash, Rachel Roy and Sara Rue, trailblazed by Demi Moore and Bruce Willis for their now grown daughter. (Trivia tidbit: Bankhead's namesake was her paternal grandmother who, in turn, was named after the Georgia town of Tallulah Falls.)

When spelled Tallula, it is also a traditional Irish name that was borne by two saints.

Tamar

Hebrew, "date palm tree"

Tamar is a rich, strong Old Testament name sometimes given to girls born on the holiday of Sukkoth, as palm branches were used to make the roof of the sukkah. In the Bible, there are several Tamars, including a daughter of King David and also Absalom's daughter, who is praised for her 'fair countenance'.

Tamar is also a river name in ancient Celtic. The River Tamar forms the border between the British counties of Devon and Cornwall, and Tamar is also associated with the Thames.

The Russian form Tamara has long outshone Tamar.

Tamsin

English, contracted form of Thomasina, "twin"

Tamsin is an offbeat name occasionally heard in Britain and just waiting to be discovered here. UK actress Tamsin Greig is a star of the show *Episodes*.

Tanaquil

tan-a-KEEL

Etruscan, "gift of God"

This intriguing name of an ancient Etruscan queen renowned for her prophetic powers was long associated with the prima ballerina Tanaquil LeClerq.

Tansy

Greek, "immortal"; English flower name; diminutive of Anastasia, Greek, "resurrection"

A flower name rarer than Rose, livelier than Lily and less teasable than Pansy.

Tassia

Diminutive of Anastasia, Greek, "resurrection"

Tassia is an obscure short form used mostly in Russia and Eastern Europe, where the name Anastasia as in the executed Russian princess is common. Rarely found in the English-speaking world, Tassia could make a distinctive and attractive nickname for this elegant royal name and can easily stand on its own.

Tay

English, diminutive of Taylor, "tailor"

Tay is occasionally used on its own, or as a nickname for the now fading Taylor.

Teal

Bird and color name

Teal is one of the prettiest and most straightforward of the new color names — an ideal middle name choice.

Temple

English, "dweller near the temple"

Temple has gained some recent notice as a girls' name via admired autistic writer Dr. Temple Grandin.

Teodora

tay-o-dor-ah

Italian, Spanish, Swedish, and Polish variation of Theodora, "gift of God"

Teodora is an extremely attractive and exotic choice, with several equally attractive, user-friendly nicknames and more edge and sheer phonic appeal than the English form, Theodora. Appealing short forms might include Tea, Dora, or Dory.

Thaïs

THA-ees

Greek, "beloved" or "bandage"

A paramour of Alexander the Great and the heroine of a Jules Massenet opera based on the life of a fourth century Egyptian saint, this name is nothing if not dramatic.

Thalassa

Greek, "the sea"

A pretty, rarely used Greek name, it usually refers to a goddess of the Mediterranean Sea. In 1991, a newly discovered moon of Neptune was dubbed Thalassa.

Thandie

South African, Xhosa, diminutive of Thandiwe, "loving one"

A captivating and sprightly name brought into the limelight by actress Thandie Newton.

Theone

Greek, "godly"

A solid, if somewhat serious Greek name. Theoni is a variant.

Thisbe

thiz-bee

Mythological name, meaning unknown

Thisbe, the name of a beautiful but tragic lover in mythology, is lively and cute — in a slightly thistly, prickly way. Ovid retold the story of Thisbe and Pyramus, young lovers kept apart by family rivalry, which was the inspiration for Romeo and Juliet. A modern bearer of the name is writer Thisbe Nissen.

Tiernan

Irish, "descendant of a lord"

An old Irish surname cousin of Tierney that makes an unusual and appealing Irish gender switch.

Tierney

Irish, "descendant of a lord"

An uncommon Irish-accented surname that seems particularly well suited to a girl. Tierney Sutton is a well-known jazz singer.

Tindra

Swedish, "to twinkle or sparkle"

Tindra is a new name in Sweden, used only since the 1980s, that has become enormously popular: It's in the Top 60 there. And while unknown in the US, Tindra certainly has possibilities as a substitute for the flagging Kendra.

Topaz

Latin gem name

As a name, Topaz is sophisticated and sultry; as a golden gem, it's said to have healing and energizing properties and also to bring good luck — and being the birthstone for November could make it perfect for a baby born in that month.

Toril

Norse, "thunder"

An unknown, strong Scandinavian name related to Tor/Thor, the Norse god of thunder, that would fit in perfectly here.

Trixie

Latin, diminutive of Beatrix, "she who brings happiness"

A sassy, spunky name for the bold parent who doesn't remember Mrs. Ed Norton on *The Honeymooners*. It was chosen by Damon Wayans for his daughter.

Tulip

Turkish, flower name

One of the most unusual flower names, Tulip is cute, but tough to pull off as a first. It has some celebrity cred via Charlie Tamara Tulip, twin daughter of Rebecca Romijn and Jerry O'Connell.

Tullia

Feminine form of Roman family name Tullius, meaning unknown

The unusual and intriguing Tullia has been used since Roman times as a feminine of the illustrious family name Tullius, as in philosopher Marcus Tullius Cicero. Modern parents who like Tallulah or Lillia but want something even more unusual would do well to consider the nearly-unknown Tullia, which may also be varied to Tulia, rhyming with Julia.

Tullia may be shortened to Tully, more properly an Irish surname with a range of possible meanings.

Tupelo

Place-name and tree name

Tupelo, the name of a Mississippi city as well as a tree with soft, light wood that grows in the swamps of the south, attracted some attention as a first name via author Tupelo Hassman. The song *Tupelo Honey* also brought it some notoriety.

U

Unity

English, "oneness"

Like Verity and Amity, this inclusive virtue name used by the colorful British literary Mitford family is ready to join its more popular peers Hope, Faith, and Grace.

V

Verity

Latin, "truth"; Virtue name

If you love Puritan virtue names and want to move beyond Hope and Faith and even Charity, this is a wonderful choice, both for its meaning and its sound. A rare find here, though occasionally used in England. It was used in Winston Graham's *Poldark* novels, was Madonna's Bond Girl name in *Die Another Day,* and made a brief appearance in *Harry Potter.*

Veronique

French form of Veronica, "true image"

Veronica seems poised to rise again, along with many other V names, and with it may follow this more romantic French version.

Vesper

Latin, "evening"

This Latin word used for evening spiritual services was introduced to baby namers by the Eva Greene character Vesper Lynd in the modern James Bond film *Casino Royale* in 2006 and is just now beginning to provoke interest among namers, with its spiritual reference and soft, whispery sound.

Vienna

Place-name: the capital of Austria

One of the most promising of the newly discovered European place-names, with a particularly pleasant sound. Possible substitute for the rapidly climbing Siena/Sienna.

Viveca

Scandinavian from Teutonic, "alive, life; place of refuge"

This is one of the most exotic and feminine of the *v*-names meaning life, and it's sure to gain more attention as the whole sisterhood of Viv- names rise. A current bearer is Swedish actress Viveca Paulin, wife of Will Ferrell.

W

Walker

English occupational name, "cloth walker"

This waspy name on the rise for boys, hasn't hit yet for girls, but could join others, like Sawyer, that have.

Wallis

Variation of Wallace, "a Welshman, Celt"

Famously borne by the woman (born Bessie) for whom an English king sacrificed his throne, Wallis has the force of a masculine name with a distinctive spelling to set it apart from the boys. Anthony Edwards revived it for his daughter, and we're hearing some buzz about it on Nameberry.

Waverly

English, "meadow of quivering aspens"

Waverly, with its literary resonance and lilting three-syllable sound, could well become the next generation's successor to Kimberly.

Spelled Waverley, this is the title of Sir Walter Scott's popular 1814 novel, whose hero is a young English soldier named Edward Waverley. Spelled the more streamlined way, Waverly is the name of the daughter of Buttercup and Wesley in *The Princess Bride* and a memorable character in *The Joy Luck Club*.

Waverly Place in Greenwich Village was named for the Scott novel in 1833, and was the setting of the teen show *The Wizards of Waverly Place*, as well as Don Draper's bachelor pad in *Mad Men*.

West

Word name

Straightforward yet romantic, this is one newly minted name with long-term appeal, especially as a middle name. It was used as such for Tea Leoni and

David Duchovny's Madelaine, whom they call West. Definitely ambigender, it was chosen by Marley Shelton for her daughter.

Whimsy

Word name

Whimsy is a new entry to the ever-expanding word name lexicon, sister for Pixie and Bliss. While it has an undeniable offbeat English aristocratic charm (maybe we're thinking of Dorothy Sayers' fictional detective Lord Peter Wimsey, whose middle name was Death?), we see this as more fitting for a middle than a first name.

Wilhelmina

German, feminine variation of Wilhelm, "resolute protection"

Until recently burdened with the Old Dutch cleanser image of thick blond braids and clunky wooden clogs, that began to change somewhat by the dynamic Vanessa Williams character on *Ugly Betty*, and even more by the choice of Wilhelmina by ace baby namers Natalie and Taylor Hanson. For the less adventurous, Willa is, for now, still a much more usable female equivalent of William.

Winslet

English surname and place-name, "Wynn's channel or stream"

Winslet is one of a legion of surnames newly considered fair game as first names. The inspiration may be British star Kate, but she's not the only reason parents are attracted to Winslet, which sounds at once classy and winning. Yet be warned that if you choose this, people will forever assume you are major fans of the actress. Other Win- beginning names up for new consideration: Winslow, Winston, Wynton, Winifred and Winnie, along with just plain Win or Wyn or Wynn.

Winslow

English, "friend's hill or burial mound"

Winslow's most famous reference may be male painter Winslow Homer, but as a name it's beginning to be on the rise for girls. Adorable nickname Winnie may be the reason. Other unusual painterly possibilities for either sex: O'Keeffe, Hopper, and just plain Painter.

Wisteria

Flower name

A frilly southern-accented flower name yet to be planted on many birth certificates. In the language of flowers, the wisteria is a symbol of devotion.

Wren

Animal name, "wren, a bird"

Wren, a lilting songbird name, could be the next Robin, and for architects there's the link to the great Sir Christopher Wren.

Wylie

Scottish, diminutive of William, "resolute protection"

Wylie is one Celtic surname with as much appeal for girls as for boys. Wylie is ripe for spelling variations: Wiley is as appropriate as Wylie but when you spell it Wylei, as Corey Parker did for his son, you're getting into yooneek naming territory.

Wynn

Welsh, "fair, pure"

Wynn is an attractive unisex Welsh name, especially worth considering as a winning middle name.

X

Xandra

ZAN-dra

Spanish, diminutive of Alexandra, "man's defender"

Like most *X*-names, pronunciation would surely be a problem for other kids, at least until they're able to say and spell xylophone.

Xanthe

ex-AHN-theh or ZAN-theh

Greek, "golden, yellow"

This Demeter-equivalent conjures up an image of an exotic, other-worldly being. It arose as a name for blondes.

Y

Yael

yah-ehl

Hebrew, "mountain goat"

Yael is an Old Testament name often heard in Israel that could work well here: just remember that it's pronounced with two syllables...and ignore the goat connection.

Yara

Arabic, "small butterfly"

The exotic Yara is also the name of a beautiful green-skinned Brazilian goddess and might make a more unusual spin on Mara or Sara.

Yardley

English surname, "wood clearing"

Yardley, a surname redolent of British soaps and perfume, was used for her daughter by Megyn Kelly.

Yeardley Smith (born Martha), has long been the voice of Bart on *The Simpsons*.

Ynez

ee-nez

Spanish variation of Agnes, "pure, virginal"

This spelling further exoticizes the lovely Inez.

Yoko

Japanese, "good girl"

There are many in Japan, but for most Americans there's only one Yoko.

Z

Zahara

Hebrew, "to shine"; Swahili, "flower"

Zahara, a delicate but strong multicultural name, came into the spotlight when Angelina Jolie bestowed it on her Ethiopian-born daughter, and we predict many other parents will adopt it as well. If you want something simpler than Zahara, consider Zara.

Zephyrine

Feminine variation of Zephyr, Greek, "west wind"

Zephyr may not be a name often heard in the U.S., but its variations are used throughout Europe. Zephyrine, a cousin in sound and feel if not in fact to such lovely names as Severine and Seraphina, has distinctive possibilities.

Zinnia

Latin Flower name

A floral choice with a bit more edge and energy than most and beginning to find its way onto namers' wish lists of botanical possibilities. Named after a German botanist called Zinn, it appears in Roald Dahl's *Matilda* as the young protagonist's mother.

Zuleika

Arabic, "brilliant and lovely"

Zuleika is a high-wire act of a name: only for the intrepid. It has a striking literary association to Max Beerbohm's Zuleika Dobson, a heroine so gorgeous that the entire student body of Oxford University killed themselves for love of her.

BOYS' NAMES

A

Abelard

German, "noble, steadfast"

Abelard brings to mind Peter/Pierre Abelard, the great twelfth century Breton scholastic philosopher and theologian, who was equally celebrated for his tragic love affair with Heloise — one of the world's most famous love stories.

This highly unusual name just might appeal to the fearless baby namer.

Abiah

Hebrew, "God is my father"

Abiah is a gentle, rarely used Old Testament name belongingto Samuel's second son. This makes a good choice for the parent who wants a traditional biblical name that is not overly familiar.

Addar

Hebrew, "mighty one"

The Biblical Addar was a son of King Bela. This obscure name is simple and strong and well-suited to modern life.

Adriano

Italian, "man from Adria"

Adriano is a dashing Italian name which gets around the possible gender confusion of Adrian.

Ajax

Greek mythology name

Ajax was the strong and courageous Greek hero featured in Homer's "Iliad," known as Ajax the Great. But it's also the name of a foaming cleanser, and if you find that reference too strong, you might try the shortened Jax instead.

Alaric

German, "all-powerful ruler"

Alaric is an ancient regal name that sounds modern enough to be considered. Alaric was a traditional name for the kings of the Ostrogoths, the most famous of whom was Alaric I, the King of the West Goths who sacked Rome in 410.

In literature, Alaric was a noble character in P. G. Wodehouse's *Blandings Castle* novels, the lead character in Alexander Theroux's *Darconville's Cat*, appeared in Stephen King's *The Dark Tower* series, and was the name of a history teacher on *The Vampire Diaries*.

More unusual than Frederic or Roderic, Alaric could make a quaintly quirky path to all the Al and Rick nicknames.

Albus

Latin, "white, bright"

The ancient name Albus has modern currency as the first name of the headmaster of Harry Potter's Hogwarts, more formally known as Professor Albus Percival Wulfric Brian Dumbledore. Can Albus work if you're missing the long white beard and the magic wand? Maybe, though it might be a heavy mantle for a Muggle child to wear.

Alistair

English spelling of Alasdair, Scottish version of Alexander, "defending warrior"

With many British names invading the Yankee name pool, the sophisticated Alistair could and should be part of the next wave. You have a triple choice with this name — the British spell it Alistair or Alastair, while the Scots prefer Alasdair — but they're all suave Gaelic versions of Alexander. Adopted by the lowland Scots by the seventeenth century, the name didn't become popular outside Scotland and Ireland until the twentieth century.

Both Andrew Lloyd-Weber and Rod Stewart chose the Alastair spelling for their sons' names.

Amedeo

Italian form of Amadeus, "lover of God"

This euphonious Italian name, often associated with the painter Modigliani, makes a recommended creative choice. The Spanish tend to spell it Amadeo.

Amias

um-EYE-us or AIM-ee-us

Latin, "loved"

Amias or Amyas is an obscure name with an attractive sound and feel and a lovely meaning. Though it might sound like a Biblical name, it is not, but is a surname that may be related to Amadeus or even be a male version of Amy — which would make it one of the few boys' names to be derived from a girls'.

The Amyas version became known via the hero of the mega-popular 1855 Charles Kingsley novel, *Westward Ho!*, Captain Sir Amyas Leigh.

Anselm

German, "with divine protection"

A somewhat solemn appellation, Anselm is a saint's name, connected to the twelfth century archbishop of Canterbury, and in modern times tied to the German neo-expressionist painter Anselm Kiefer.

Ara

Arabic, "rainmaker"; Armenian, "handsome"; Hebrew, "lion"

Ara is one of the most melodious in the Armenian name pool, familiarized by Notre Dame football coach Ara Parseghian. This multi-origined name has new possibilities thanks to such high-profile personalities with similar feeling names as young actor Asa Butterfield of *Hugo* and character Ari Gold on *Entourage*.

Aragon

Spanish place name

Equally strong, dramatic and romantic, this name of an old kingdom in the Iberian Peninsula and a modern Spanish community as well, would give a boy an instant pedigree.

Aram

Hebrew, "high elevated"

Aram is a popular Armenian name with a pleasing sound that became known in this country through the works of William Saroyan, namely the 1940 book of short stories, *My Name is Aram*, centering on Aram Garoghlanian, a boy of Armenian descent growing up in Fresno, California. Saroyan also named his son Aram.

Aram appears in the bible as a son of Shem and grandson of Noah; it is also a biblical place name. In addition, Aram is the third day of the month in the Armenian calendar.

A well known bearer is Aram Khachaturian, the Armenian composer.

Aristotle

Greek, "superior"

The great philosopher's name is commonly used in Greek families, and is one that could work for daring, exotically inclined American ones.

Arjan

Dutch, variation of Hadrian, "from Hadria" ; Punjabi

There's something particularly attractive about names with an interior "j" and Arjan is a prime example. The Punjabi version is pronounced with a conventional j as in jar; the Dutch Arjan, which is a variation of Adrien, pronounces the 'j' like a 'y'. Another Dutch version is Arje.

Arkady

Russian from Greek, "from Arcadia"

Arkady is a rhythmic Russian saint's name from the Greek meaning "from Arcadia." As a literary name, it belongs to a genteel character in Turgenev's *Fathers and Sons* and a much less benign one in Dostoyevsky's *Crime and Punishment*, and is also a key figure in *Gorky Park* by Martin Cruz Smith.

Armistead

English, "hermit's place"

This dignified Old English surname was brought into the modern consciousness by author Armistead Maupin, who wrote the San Francisco stories *Tales of the City*. There was also a Civil War general named Lewis Armistead.

Arpad

Hungarian, "seed"

Arpad is a hero name in Hungary, belonging to the Second Grand Prince of the Maygars, who established a dynasty that ruled for four centuries. Not heard often here, but is associated with the French-born financier who got his name from an earlier Hungarian banker and who's been involved with two of the world's most beautiful women — he is, in fact the father of Rosalind Arusha Arkadina Altalune Florence Thurman-Busson.

Arrow

Word name

Words are not always easy to translate into baby names, but the implications of being straight and swift lend this one great potential as a name. It also has the popular *o*-sound ending, which brings it further into the realm of possibility. Rising rock star Aja Volkman pulled a gender switch when she named her daughter Arrow Eve.

Asaiah

Hebrew, "the Lord hath made"

Asaiah is a name found several times in the Old Testament. Think of it as a blend of Asa and Josiah and a possible substitute for Isaiah.

Ash

Diminutive of Asher, English, "ash tree"

Ash has Southern charm plus the arboreal-nature appeal. Plus your little boy will prize Ash as the name of the hero of the "Pokemon" cartoons. Ash can also be a dashing short form of Asher, Ashton, or any other Ash- name, except Ashley, which we'll now leave to the girls.

Auberon

English from German, "noble, bearlike"

Rarely heard in the US, Auberon has a gentle autumnal feel rare in a male name. Possibly starting as a pet form of Aubrey, it was also infuenced by Oberon, the king of the fairies in Shakespeare's *A Midsummer Night's Dream*.

The most famous bearer of the name is British journalist and critic Auberon Waugh (whose grandfather was Aubrey), of the literary Waugh clan.

The Oberon spelling is another recommended option.

Aubin

French form of Alban, "white, blond"

More appealing than the English version, Aubin might be seen as a fresher and more masculine twist on Aubrey.

Auden

English, "old friend"

The poetic, soft-spoken Auden has recently started to be considered as a first name option, used for both sexes, appreciated for its pleasing sound as well as its link to the distinguished modern Anglo-American poet W.H. Auden.

Augusten

German variation of Augustus, Augustine, Augustin, "great, magnificent"

Confessional memoirist Augusten Burroughs is the first literary notable to bear one of this family of names since the confessional saint.

Aurelius

Latin, "the golden one"

Since Aurelius was given the supermodel seal of approval by Elle Macpherson, this is one of the Roman emperor names, like Augustus, now in the realm of possibility. Like the female Aurelia and Aurora, Aurelius has a particularly warm golden aura.

In ancient Roman history, the name is associated with Marcus Aurelius, a Roman Emperor from 161 to 180 AD, the last of the so-called "Five Good Emperors." He is also considered one of the most important Stoic philosophers.

Averill

English, "boar battle"

Averill is an ancient name, most properly spelled Averil, that has a Boston Brahmin air — probably due to the image of statesman Averill Harriman — but it does feel a tad feminine in this era of Avas and Averys.

Azarias

Hebrew, variation of Azariah, "God has helped"

This is another form of the name the angel Raphael assumes for himself when he becomes human. One of the few attractive Biblical names that has not yet been discovered by modern parents, Azarias is certainly ripe for the taking.

B

Bairam

Turkish, "festival"

Though Bairam is not well known in the U.S., it's a name that easily crosses cultures because it sounds exactly like the English name Byram, a variation of Byron. Bairam is the name of two Mohammedan festivals, one that ends Ramadan and one that takes place 70 days later. Like Felix and Asher, Bairam is a name with a happy, uplifting meaning.

Baird

Scottish occupational name, "minstrel, poet"

Meaning bard, this is an original choice with poetic and melodic undertones. Bard itself has also come into consideration, both names bringing to mind Shakespeare and other literary lights.

The Scottish surname Baird's most notable bearer was John Logie Baird, the Scottish engineer and inventor of the televisor, the world's first practical television system in 1926, and also the world's first fully electronic color TV tube two years later. Some might also remember puppeteers Bil and Cora Baird.

Balthazar

Phoenician, "Baal protects the King"

This evocative name of one of the Three Wise Men of the Orient, also spelled Balthasar, may finally be ready for prime time. Balthazar, Melchior and Caspar were the Magi who brought gifts of gold, frankincense and myrrh to the baby Jesus, though their names were not mentioned in the Bible.

Balthazar, in its various spellings, has been attached to a number of distinguished artists, writers and philosophers of the past; the most prominent contemporary bearer is Balthazar Getty, actor and great-grandson of J. Paul Getty. The iconoclastic modern painter Balthus was born Balthasar.

Balthazar is well represented in literature. The name appears in no fewer than four Shakespeare plays, is the title of a Lawrence Durrell novel, is the main character of a Balzac novel, and has been seen in everything from a James Bond film to *Buffy the Vampire Slayer* to *The Smurfs* to *Xbox* and online games, and there is a J. P. Donleavy novel titled *The Beastly Beatitudes of Balthazar B.*

Bardo

German saint name; also Aboriginal, "water"

Bardo has a poetic beginning and upbeat ending. Saint Bardo was the eleventh century bishop of Mainz, in Germany, which may be one reason Sandra Bullock (whose mother was German) chose the name as her son's middle. Bardo is also a Tibetan concept of an intermediate state. Bullock's choice inevitably shines a spotlight on this obscure name.

Barnabas

Aramaic, "son of consolation"

Barnabas, whose birth name was Joseph, was one of the earliest Christian disciples in Jerusalem, who undertook missionary journeys with Paul the Apostle, His name is a bit Old World compared to the update Barnaby, but could gain some attention as boys' names ending in 's' are enjoying a comeback.

Barnaby

English variation of Barnabas, Aramaic, "son of consolation"

Barnaby, a genial and energetic name with an Irish-sounding three-syllable lilt, is an ancient appellation that manages to be both unusual and highly attractive and deserves to be used more than it is. A sweet-spot name that's a real winner.

Barnaby is a version of Barnabas, the name of an Apostle companion of St. Paul on his missionary journeys. The name of the good-natured hero of Dickens's novel *Barnaby Rudge*, it became more familiar to the modern American public through the TV series *Barnaby Jones*. Barnaby has been a character in *Hello, Dolly!*, a doctor played by Cary Grant in the movie *Monkey Business*, a comic strip character, and has starred in a number of children's books.

Basie

Scottish surname, meaning unknown

Basie is a fabulous jazz name to honor the Count, whose birth name was

William, the influential pianist, organist, bandleader and composer who led his band for almost fifty years.

There are lots of other jazzy names you might want to consider, including Ellington, Miles, Quincy, Dexter, Mercer, and Bix. Woody Allen named his two daughters after jazz musicians: Bechet for clarinetist Sidney Bechet and Manzie for Manzie Johnson, the drummer in Bechet's band.

Bastian

Diminutive of Sebastian, Latin from Greek, "man of Sebastia"
In Spanish cultures, and spelled either Bastian or Bastien, this is a fairly common nickname name. The German fantasy children's book *The Neverending Story* features a young boy character called Bastian Balthazar Bux, and it has also been seen in several screen versions.

Bastian has been enjoying recent popularity in Latin America: it reached Number 11 in Chile — as well as in Germany and Scandinavia, and is just beginning to be appreciated here. Jeremy Sisto used it for his son.

Alternate spelling Bastien is also a fashionable Euro form with a possible future in America. There is a one-act comic opera by Mozart titled *Bastien and Bastienne*.

Baz

Diminutive of Sebastian, "man of Sebastia" or Basil, "regal"
As Bas, it's a popular name in The Netherlands, but Baz, as in director Luhrmann, has potential for independent life too.

Curiously, Australian-born *Moulin Rouge* director Luhrmann was born neither Sebastian nor Basil, but had the name Mark Anthony on his birth certificate; his nickname arose from his supposed resemblance to a British TV fox puppet named Basil Brush.

Beech

English, "beech tree"
If you prefer the woods to the ocean, you might want to name your son (or daughter) Beech instead of Beach.

Benigno

ben-NEEN-yo

Latin, "kind, wellborn"

From the root that gives us "benign," Benigno is not as accessible in English-speaking cultures as such names as Bruno and Benicio. Filipino Senator Benigno Aquino, Jr., went by his nickname Ninoy.

Benno

German, "bear"

Benno is a cool name in its own right — there was a tenth century Saint Benno — though it is also used as a lively nickname for Benjamin. Saint Benno of Meissen is the patron saint of anglers and weavers and, strangely enough, alliteration.

Benno came to attention in the U.S. via the father and son duo of Benno Schmidt Sr. and Jr. Senior was the venture capitalist who invented the term venture capitalist and Junior was the president of Yale University. Benno is also the appellation of a student character in Umberto Eco's *The Name of the Rose.*

Bingham

British surname, "homestead at a hollow"

Bingham is the unusual surname name chosen by Kate Hudson and Matt Bellamy for their son. It was Bellamy's mother's maiden name, and the nickname Bing, coincidentally, belongs to almost-stepfather Kurt Russell's dad. We haven't heard Bing since crooner Crosby, but it does have a lot of zing.

Ryan Bingham is the name of the George Clooney character in *Up in the Air.*

Birch

Tree name

Birch is a rarely used nature name that calls to mind the lovely image of the tall, strong but graceful white-barked tree.

The best known bearer of the name is former high-ranking Democratic Senator Birch Evans Bayh, who carried the name of his father and was the principal Senate sponsor of the Equal Rights Amendment.

The birch tree has many notable qualities and uses — including the making of furniture, paper, canoes, and drums, is considered the national tree of Russia (where it used to be worshiped as a goddess), the state tree of New Hampshire, and has spiritual significance in several cultures.

Bix

Modern nickname

Bix is a cool and jazzy nickname name, thanks to that final x. It's largely associated with the legendary and influential cornet player (and inspiration for the novel *Young Man With a Horn*), Bix Beiderbecke. He was born Leon Bismark Beiderbecke and his nickname derived from his middle name.

Bix could easily fit in with cousins Jax, Dax, etc.

Boaz

Hebrew, "swiftness"

Now that such Old Testament patriarchs as Elijah and Moses fill the playground, Boaz seems downright baby-friendly, having more pizzazz than many of the others, perhaps as a successor to Noah.

A name that was used by the seventeenth century Pilgrims and is still heard in Israel, but is a rarity in the U.S., Boaz is associated with the Jewish holiday Shavuot, as that is when the Bible story of Ruth is read in the synagogue, and Boaz was Ruth's wealthy and generous second husband, making it logical for Boaz to sometimes be given to boys born at that time.

Extra added attraction: one of the all-time great nicknames — Bo.

Bram

Dutch variation of Abraham, "father of multitudes"

Bram has an unusual measure of character and charm for a one-syllable name; it started as a hipper-than-Abe diminutive of the biblical Abraham, but is also an independent Irish and Dutch name, made famous by Irish-born Dracula creator Bram (nee Abraham) Stoker. Bram is currently Number 16 in the Netherlands; Bram Howard was a character on *The West Wing*.

Another route to Bram is Bramwell, as in early actor Bramwell Fletcher, who — speaking of horror movies — was noted for his mad scenes in the 1932 film *The Mummy*.

Bran

Diminutive of Brandon, "broom-covered hill"

A little heavy on the fiber content; we prefer Bram. But Bran is also the Celtic god of the underworld, whose symbol is the raven.

Brenner

German, "to burn"

Brenner is an occupational surname for both a charcoal burner and a distiller of spirits. One of the least used of occupational surnames, it has that 'er' ending that definitely adds to its stylishness; a possible successor to Brendan.

Brick

Word name, various origins

This is an Anglicized form of various names; the Irish Gaelic O Bruic; German, Bruck or Breck, meaning "swamp" or "wood"; Yiddish, Brik, "bridge"; and Slovenian, Bric, "dweller from a hilly place." Gosh, and we thought it was just a macho word name invented by Tennessee Williams for the hero of *Cat on a Hot Tin Roof.*

C

Cabot

French, "to sail"

Cabot is an attractive English surname associated with the daring early Italian-born British explorer known as John Cabot; his birth name was Giovanni Caboto.

Cadmus

Greek, "from the east" or "one who excels"

Cadmus is the name of the serpent-slaying hero of Greek mythology who also founded the city of Thebes and is credited with inventing the alphabet. Its ancient feel might appeal to modern parents — especially since Cadmus Peverell is a human *Harry Potter* character, one of the three original owners of the Deathly Hallows.

Caius

Latin, "rejoice"; variation of Gaius

Caius is classical and serious but also has a simple, joyful quality. There was a third century pope named Caius, as well as an early Christian writer, several Shakespearean characters, and a *Twilight* vampire. We would pronounce the name to rhyme with eye-us though at Cambridge University in England, where it's the name of a college, it's pronounced keys. Nickname Cai is a definite asset.

Calixto

cah-LEEKS-toe

Greek, "beautiful"

Calixto is known in Spain as the name of three popes, one of whom was the martyr, Calixtus I, regarded as a saint. Calixto has a lot of energy and futuristic spirit, thanks in part to the attention-grabbing 'x.' He is the main character in the Spanish classic, Fernando de Rojas's *Tragicomedy of Calixto and Melibea.*

Callahan

Irish, "descendent of Ceallachan," "bright-headed"

Callahan, the phonetic spelling of Callaghan, is a rhythmic jig of a name whose history harks back to the ancient King of Munster. In the *Dirty Harry* movies, the Clint Eastwood character is Harry Callahan.

Callaway

Irish from Latin, "pebbly place"

Another animated Irish surname, this one with jazzy ties to the immortal "Dean of American Jive," Cab Calloway.

Carver

English, "wood carver"

Carver is an occupational name with an artistic bent, as is the newly arrived Painter, which has a fresher feel than the 1990's Carter. It also has eminent last-name links to botanist and educator George Washington Carver and short story master Raymond Carver.

Carver appears as a character in the R. D. Blackmore classic *Lorna Doone*.

Cashel

KAH-hal or CASH-ill

Irish, "castle, stone fort"

The Gaelic Cashel was chosen by actor Daniel Day-Lewis and his writer-director wife Rebecca Miller for their son.

In Ireland, Cashel refers to a circular stone fort. It is the name of a town in Tipperary and the protagonist of the George Bernard Shaw novel *Cashel Byron's Profession*.

The Cash sound feels especially contemporary and appealing now, with Cashel joining such stylish brothers as Cassius, Cassian, and Cash.

Caspar

Persian, variation of Gaspar, "keeper of the treasure"

After half a century, this otherwise feasible name has at last started to lose its link to the friendly ghost; it certainly didn't scare model Claudia Schiffer, who chose it for her son, as did Atomic Kitten Jenny Frost. Iconoclastic namer Jason Lee switched genders and called his daughter Casper. Also related to the revived Jasper, Caspar seems headed towards the path to a similar resurgence.

Caspar is the name of one of the Three Magi who brought gifts to the infant Jesus — Caspar of Tarsus was the one who brought the gift of gold.

In the Casper spelling, the name was quite popular in the US near the end of the nineteenth century, peaking in 1889 at Number 332, but it dropped off the list completely in 1933. It still retains its popularity in Scandinavia and Belgium.

Actor Casper van Dien was the tenth generation in his family to bear the name of his Dutch ancestors, continuing the tradition with his son Casper Robert Mitchum.

Caspian

Place name
One of the most romantic of appellations, as well as being a geographical name of the large salty sea between Asia and Europe that probably inspired C.S. Lewis to use it for the name of the hero of his children's novel, *Prince Caspian*, part of the *Chronicles of Narnia* series.

Caspian is attracting a lot of attention from cutting-edge parents these days.

Cassian

Latin, variation of Cassius, "hollow"
Cassian is a saints' and Latin clan name, related to Cassius, that is virtually unused and waiting to be discovered.

There have been at least four fourth and fifth century St. Cassians, one of whom is the patron saint of (not many of them left) stenographers. John Cassian was a monk and ascetic writer who introduced Eastern monasticism into the West.

Patrick Wilson used the alternate spelling Kassian for his son.

Cathan

Irish, "little battler"
Cathan is one Irish boys' name that remains underused and would be an intriguing way to honor an ancestral Catherine. It is related to Cain and, theoretically, the nouveau Cayden.

Cayo

Latin, from the Roman family name Caius, "rejoice"
Cayo is a rare and rhythmic Spanish name, all but unknown in the English-speaking world, that would make a lively choice.

Cedar

English, tree name

Cedar is, like Ash, Oak, Pine and Ebony, one of the new tree/wood names that parents are starting to consider; this one is particularly aromatic.

In the Bible the cedar is mentioned in Psalm 92:12: "The righteous shall flourish like the palm tree and grow like a cedar in Lebanon." The Lebanon Cedar was used to build King Solomon's temple in Jerusalem, and there are now several hospitals called Cedars of Lebanon, plus a U2 song by that name.

A contemporary bearer of the name is the jazz pianist Cedar Walton.

Chaplin

English, "clergyman of a chapel"

Chaplin carries two very distinctive images: the beloved Little Tramp and a minister, often to the military. It was the baby-name choice of Ever Carridine in 2010.

Christo

Slavic, "one who carries Christ"

This unusual name, which is jauntier than Chris when used as a diminutive of Christopher, is associated with the Bulgarian installation artist of that name, responsible for wrapping many public institutions and known especially for *The Gates of Central Park* and *Running Fence*. Christo is his full given name.

Ciaran

KEER-awn

Irish, "little black-haired one"

Extremely popular in Ireland, Ciaran is also well used in England and is beginning to infiltrate the U.S., more popularly with the phonetic Kieran spelling. An all-around attractive name whose only mild downside might be its similarity to the outmoded female Karen.

Although it was the name of twenty-six saints in Ireland, Ciaran was not used as a secular name there until the 1950s, and then more often in the Anglicized form, Kieran.

Belfast-born actor Ciaran Hinds played Aberforth Dumbledore in *Harry Potter and the Deathly Hollows*.

Cillian

KIL-yan

Irish, "war, strife"

This Irish classic, which is better known in this country by its phonetic form Killian, is one of several newer recommended Gaelic choices that have entered the American name pool. Killian now stands at Number 756, while Cillian is 22 in its Irish homeland.

There are several Saint Cillians, including one who was sent to Bavaria to convert the natives and was martyred for his trouble. The best known contemporary bearer of the name in versatile actor Cillian Murphy.

Clancy

Irish, "red-haired warrior"

Clancy, one of the original crossover Irish surname names, is as energetic and appealing as ever — full of moxie, more distinctive than Casey, and also one of the less obvious of the red-headed names.

A literary namesake is Clancy Sigel, author of the autobiographical novel *Going Away*, and there is also the comical mid-century song, *Clancy Lowered the Boom*.

More common as a last name than a first, Clancy has gained fame via the Irish folk music group the Clancy Brothers, and one of the bestselling authors of all time, Tom Clancy, known for his espionage and techno thrillers.

Colm

Irish variation of Latin Columba, "dove"

Colm is a popular boys' name in Ireland that could immigrate, especially with its peaceful meaning. Colm Toibin is a contemporary Irish novelist and critic, author of *The Master and Brooklyn*; Colm Meaney is an Irish actor. Pronunciation is two syllables instead of one, like Colin with an '*m*' at the end. Colm is related to Columba, Colom, Colum, Callum - — and Malcolm.

Coltrane

Irish surname

The great sax player John Coltrane could be a cool naming inspiration for a jazz fan.

Conan

Irish, "little wolf"

The fierce image of the Barbarian made a complete turnaround thanks to amiable talk show host O'Brien, making Conan one of the newly desirable Irish choices, a perfect alternative to Conor/Connor.

In Gaelic, Conan was the name of an illustrious seventh-century Irish saint, bishop of the Isle of Man. Sherlock Holmes creator Arthur Conan Doyle was born in Scotland, of Irish stock.

Connery

Irish, "warrior-lord"

This appealing name of a mythical king of Tara whose reign brough prosperity to his kingdom is strongly associated with actor Sean. The Irish form is Conaire.

Constantin

Latin, "steadfast"

More likely to be spelled Constantine, this was the name of the first Christian emperor of the Roman empire, as well as three Scottish kings. Previously thought of as too bulky and unwieldy a name for a modern child, these days it would be perfectly acceptable.

Cord

Diminutive of Cordell, "maker or seller of rope or cord"

This is the kind of strong one-syllable boy's name many parents are seeking these days. The more musical Chord was introduced by hot young actor Chord Overstreet.

Corentin

kor-en-TAN

French, Breton, "tempest, hurricane"

Corentin is an intriguing saint's name fashionable in France but virtually unknown here — which you may consider a big plus. St. Corentin possessed a magical fish that regenerated itself each night, feeding himself and his lucky visitors in perpetuity.

Corin

Latin, "spear"

Corin was used by Shakespeare in *As You Like It*, an unusual name that could make a more distinctive alternative to Corey or Colin. It is a name used in the illustrious Redgrave family of actors.

Cormac

Irish, "charioteer"; Greek, "tree trunk"

Both offbeat and upbeat, this evocative traditional Irish name that runs through Celtic mythology is known here via award-winning novelist Cormac McCarthy (born Charles). The author's adopted name is related to Cormac Mac Airt, one of the great legendary high kings of Ireland.

In two of the *Harry Potter* movies, Cormac McLaggen is a Gryffindor student.

And for all you popularity-phobes, Cormac, like the rest of the names in this book, has never yet made it onto the American Top 1000 list.

Cosimo

Italian variation of Cosmo, "universe"

Dramatic, worldly, and exotic, Cosimo was chosen by singer Beck and his wife, Marissa Ribisi, for their son. Now that Cosima has emerged as a starbaby favorite, twin brother Cosimo could join her.

Cosimo de Medici was the first of the Medici dynasty to wield power in Florence during much of the Italian Renaissance, and was noted for his patronage of the arts. An inspirational name for creative parents.

Crane

English surname, "crane"

This elegant surname has great potential to turn into an unusual first name, especially with its literary associations to both Stephen and Hart Crane.

Crane is a surname that originated for a tall man with long, thin legs. It can now be seen as one of the newly stylish bird name, like Wren and Lark, and could fit in well with future classmates Zane, Kane, Dane, Lane, Rain — and Jane.

Crispin

Latin, "curly-haired"

Crispin, which was introduced into the mainstream by actor Crispin Glover and which means "curly-haired" in Latin, has an image very much like its first syllable: crisp, autumnal, and colorful.

St. Crispin, the patron saint of shoemakers, died in the third century and, as rousingly referenced by Shakespeare, Henry V fought a great battle on St. Crispin's Day. Crispin Glover was actually named for the Shakespearean speech.

In the *Harry Potter* books, Crispin Cronk is an egyptophile wizard who kept several sphinxes in his backyard.

Crispian is an interesting, rarely used variation, as is Crispus, associated with African-American hero Crispus Atticus, the first colonist to die for independence in the Boston Massacre.

Curran

Irish surname from O Corrain, "descendant of Curran"

Curran is a common surname in Ireland, but unusual even there as a first. With its savory feel, calling to mind curry and currants, Curran can make for an attractive update of Colin or Connor.

D

Dash

Diminutive of Dashiell, meaning unknown

Dash is a nickname that can stand on its own and sounds, well, dashing. Connected these days with Kardashian enterprises.

Dashiell

DASH-el

Anglicization of French surname de Chiel, meaning unknown

Dashiell, though missing from many other name sources, is among the hottest new names, chosen by such celebs as Cate Blanchett and author Helen (*Bridget Jones*) Fielding. With its great dash and panache, Dashiell is associated with detective writer Dashiell Hammett (born Samuel, as in Sam Spade, Dashiell being his mother's maiden name). Alice Cooper was ahead of the game: He named his son Dashiell in 1985.

The young animated superhero in *The Incredibles* is Dashiell 'Dash' Parr.

And Dash is such a dashing nickname.

Dennison

English, "son of Dennis"

A case in which the son is now more attractive than the father. There have been Colonial settlers surnamed Dennison on this side of the Atlantic since 1623.

Dermot

Irish, Anglicization of Diarmaid, "free man" or "free from envy"

Dermot is an appealing, relatively undiscovered Irish mythological hero's name long popular in the Old Country, and imported into the American consciousness by actor Dermot Mulroney. We see it in the next Celtic wave following Connor and Liam.

The name Dermot was borne by several early kings and a number of saints, as well as the legendary king of Tara. A further plus: The legendary Diarmaid (pronounced DEER-mit), a member of the band of Finn MacCool, had a mark on his face that caused women to fall instantly and madly in love with him.

Kermit the Frog owes his name to a regional variant of Dermot.

Dex

Diminutive of Dexter, "dyer; right-handed"

Dex, the nickname for Dexter that is sometimes used on its own, has lots of energy and sex appeal. It was chosen by comedian Dana Carvey for his now grown son. With the growing popularity of Dexter, we may be seeing more of Dex.

There are no less than three video game characters named Dex, and the leading male figure in the movie *One Day* is known by his nickname Dex. Way back in TV's *Dynasty* era, there was a character redundantly named Dex Dexter.

Django

JANG-oh

Gypsy, "I awake"

Django — the *D* is silent as most everyone now knows — the nickname of the great Belgian-born jazz guitarist Django (originally Jean Baptiste) Reinhardt, makes a dynamic musical choice for any jazz aficionado. Reinhardt's nickname "Django" is Romani for "I awake." The name has become more familiar with the release of and acclaim for the Quentin Tarantino film *Django Unchained.*

Donahue

Irish, "dark fighter"

This genial Irish surname feels much more current than Donald.

Donnelly

Irish, "dark, brave one"

Donnelly is among the more appealing Irish surname names, less well used than Donovan. Related options include the place name Donegal and the mythological god name Donegan.

Dougal

Scottish, "dark stranger"

Heard in the Scottish highlands, and much more in tune with the present times than the dated Douglas — for which it could make a perfect tribute name. Dougal was the Scottish nickname for invading dark-haired Danish Vikings, just as Fingal was given to the blonder Norwegians.

Dougray, as in actor Dougray Scott, is a similarly appealing choice.

Dov

Hebrew, "bear"

Fierce meaning, gentle image. This name is very common in Israel, where an endearing pet form is Dubi.

Drummer

Occupational word name

Drummer entered the baby name lexicon thanks to blogger No Big Dill, who chose it for her newborn son, who joins five older sisters. Drummer is right in step with other occupational names in vogue now, from Archer to Gardener. Let's just hope Drummer doesn't prefer to play the piano.

Dugan

Irish, "swarthy"

Dugan is an open, friendly, and cheery Irish surname that would be suited to a dark-haired boy.

Durant

Latin, "enduring"

Durant's meaning signifies staying power, a good quality to impart to your child. Notables with the surname Durant include Pulitzer Prize-winning authors Will and Ariel Durant, most famous for their eleven-volume *The Story of Civilization*, and William Crappo Durant, co-founder of General Motores and Chevrolet.

E

Eames

English, "son of the uncle"

An upscale surname with a nice modern design connection to the creators of the Eames chair and other midcentury furniture classics, Charles and Ray Eames.

Eamon

AY-mon

Irish variation of Edmund, "rich protector"

This Irish name pronounced ay-mon was popularized in the US by early president of the independent republic Eamon de Valera (birth name George), who was born in the United States to an Irish mother and a Cuban father. Eamon definitely has possibilities as a successor to the epidemically popular Aidan/Aiden.

Though it may be an older generation name in Ireland, it would sound fresh elsewhere.

The original spelling of the name is Eamonn.

Eban

Hebrew, diminutive of Ebenezer, "stone of help"

Affable and creative and perfectly able to stand alone; there's nothing Scroogish about it, even though it is usually spelled Eben.

Egan

Ee-ghin or Ay-ghin

Irish, pet form of Aiden, "little fire"

Egan's likeness to the word eager gives this Irish surname a ready-to-please, effervescent energy, and it would make an appropriate substitute for the overused Aidan.

This popular Irish surname originated in County Tipperary.

Egan O'Rahilly (born Aogan O Raithaille) was the outstanding poet of his age, specializing in the vision poem, or aisling, in which he told of prophesies that Ireland would triumph over her enemies. In folklore, this Egan is depicted as a wise trickster.

Eleazer

Variation of Lazarus, "God helps"

Four-syllable names can be tricky, but this rarely used Old Testament appellation has considerable potential. In the Bible, Eleazer is a son of Aaron and nephew of Moses who succeeds his father as High Priest.

Elia

Italian variation of Elijah, "Jehovah is God"

A multicultural appellation, found in Hebrew, Italian, and Zuni, this likable name made famous by director Elia Kazan's only problem is the feminine *a*-ending. But then again, that never hurt Joshua.

Elio

Italian and Spanish from Greek sun god, Helios

Elio is a sunny and spirited Italian and Spanish name that makes a great crossover prospect, which could catch on as Enzo has. Elio is also currently popular in France, ranking in the Top 250.

Ellington

English place name and surname, "Ellis's town"

Ellington is a swinging musical name, evoking the jazzy and elegant persona of the Duke (born Edward Kennedy Ellington). While that reference may seem to make Ellington a male name, it is also occasionally used for girls.

Ellington is the winning middle name of Cynthia Nixon's son Max.

Eoin

o-wen

Irish, variation of John, "God is gracious"

Though Eoin is a Gaelic form of John, its Anglicized pronunciation links it directly to Owen. Eoin is currently a Top 30 name in Ireland. Other variations: Ewan, Ewen, Evan and Eoghan (pronounced as Owen but also translated as Eugene).

Eoin Colfer is the author of the *Artemis Fowl* books.

Esai

EE-sye or ee-SAY

Spanish from Hebrew, "wealthy" or "gift"

This Hebrew-Latin name, which bristles with electricity, is associated with Esai Morales, who is a junior, carrying on his father's name.

Esmond

English, "graceful protection"

Though slightly haughtier and less accessible than cousin Edmond, Esmond could appeal to some parents seeing a distinguished appellation. It began being used (albeit sparingly) in England in the nineteenth century, possibly influenced by William Makepeace Thackeray's novel *The History of Henry Esmond.*

Etienne

French variation of Stephen, "garland, crown"

It's the French Steve yet feels oh so much more debonair. Well-used and still a popular classic in French-speaking lands, but nearly unknown to English speakers, except maybe fashionistas who associate it with designer Etienne Aigner. A new way to honor Grandpa Steve?

Ewan

YOO-un

Scottish form of Gaelic Eoghann, "youth"

This appealing name has a good chance of catching on due to the popularity of Ewan McGregor, and the trend towards Gaelic names in general. Pronunciation is YOO-un.

Ewan has a complex family tree, with connections to John, Owen, Hugh, Evan and Eugene. Other spellings are Ewen, Eoin and Euan.

In Willa Cather's novel *My Mortal Enemy*, there is a character called Ewan Gray.

Ezio

Eyh-tzee-o

Italian from Greek, "eagle"

An operatic Italian option via *South Pacific* star Pinza, one of several Italian names currently hot in France.

F

Faulkner

English, "falconer"

Faulkner is an old occupational surname that was used for someone who kept and trained falcons when falconry was a popular sport in medieval Europe. Anyone using it in contemporary America would probably be honoring Southern novelist William Faulkner. While we love the author, Falconer would probably be a slightly easier name to carry on the playground.

Fenno

A Finnish tribe and language

Fenno, a name we'd never heard before or since, was the hero of the acclaimed Julia Glass novel, *Three Junes* — an interesting new discovery.

Fergus

Scottish and Irish, "man of force"

In Celtic lore, Fergus was the ideal of manly courage; Fergus is a charming, slightly quirky Scottish and Irish favorite.

As a name, Fergus forms a link between Ireland and Scotland, as Gaelic tradition has it that Irish Prince Fergus Mac Eirc and his two brothers crossed the sea and founded the kingdom of Argyll in Scotland, thereby making this an excellent choice for parents of either or a combined heritage.

Fergus has often popped up in children's literature, such as in *Thomas the Tank Engine and Friends*, and is the name of one of Shrek and Fiona's triplets. On a loftier level, there is the Yeats poem, *Who Goes With Fergus?*

With the nickname Fergie having been appropriated by two high-profile females, we'd opt for using Gus instead.

Field

Nature name

More unusual than Forest or Forrest, Field is a nature name that is simple, evocative, and fresh — sort of the male equivalent of Meadow.

Field and Fields are both relatively common surnames, noted bearers including department store owner Marshall Field, poet Eugene Field (*Wynken, Blynken and Nod*) and actress Sally. Those with the plural include W.C. Fields, cookie company founder Debbi, and entertainers Gracie and Kim Fields.

Fielding is a very usable extension.

Finbar

Irish, "fair-haired"

This is an ancient saints' name well used in Ireland but a rarity here and unlikely to ever reach the popularity of other Finn-ish names. St. Finbarr (the more common spelling) is the patron saint of Cork and in Irish folklore, Finbarr was king of the fairies.

Finnian

Irish, "fair"

Finnian is a fair jig of a name, energetic and easy on the ear. Finnian (and brother Finian) is also familiar in its alternate spelling through the classic 1968 Broadway musical *Finian's Rainbow*, later made into a film starring Fred Astaire as Finian McLonergan.

There is also a St. Finnian who was a famous teacher and scholar.

We think Finnian/Finian could really catch on in the wake of cousins Finn and Finlay/Finley.

Fitzwilliam

English, "son of William"

The Christian name of the dashing Mr. Darcy in *Pride and Prejudice* — it was his mother's maiden name — is just one of several Fitz names, including Fitzroy, Fitzgerald, Fitzpatrick, that could be used to honor a dad named William, Roy, Gerald or Patrick.

Flanagan

Irish, "red, ruddy"

Flanagan is an elaboration of Flann, and cousin of Flynn and Finn: a member of the family of colorful Irish red-headed names. This one is lively and undiscovered.

Florin

French and Romanian form of Ancient Roman Florinus, "flower"

Florin is one of the legion of names derived from the root word for flower, most of them like Flora and Florence used for girls. But the boys' form Florin is popular in France, along with sister name Flore. There was a ninth century Swiss St. Florin. The related Florian was the name of a second century Roman saint.

The florin was an old coin which now survives in videogames.

Forster

English, variation of Foster, "scissors maker"

Forster, a variation of Foster or potentially even Forester, is associated with British novelist E.M. Forster, author of *A Passage to India, Howard's End*, and *A Room with a View*. But if you choose Forster, you'd always have to force that 'r'.

Fox

Animal name

Fox is one animal name backed by a longish tradition, and then popularized via the lead character Fox Mulder on *X Files*. Fox is simple, sleek, and a little bit wild, and could make an interesting middle name.

It was reported that the TV character's first name was not a tribute to the Fox network which aired *The X-Files*, as often assumed; show creator Chris Carter said he had a childhood friend named Fox.

Frost

English surname, "white-haired, born in a cold spell"

Long heard as a last name, as in venerable poet Robert, UK talk show host David, British actress Sadie and old Jack Frost, the personification of cold winter weather, Frost has suddenly entered the scene as a possible first, along with other seasonal weather names like Winter and Snow.

Some forward-thinking parents are beginning to warm to the icy simplicity of Frost.

G

Gable

French, "triangular feature in architecture"

The iconic *Gone With the Wind* star Clark's surname was brought into the first-name mix when *Weeds'* Kevin Nealon picked it for his son. Gable makes a strong and unusual possibility, a rhyming cousin to Abel and Mable.

The cast of Golden Age and later Hollywood character names is ever increasing, now including Harlow, Chaplin, Flynn and Monroe.

Gallagher

Irish, "descendant of foreign helper"

Gallagher is, like so many of its genre, friendly, open, and optimistic. Some might associate it with the fraternal members of the band Oasis — Noel and Liam Gallagher.

Galway

Place-name

Associated with the poet and novelist Galway Kinnell, this name of an Irish town, county, and bay would make an evocative choice. For further literary cred, writers Liam O'Flaherty and Frank Harris both hail from Galway.

Galway has several sister cities in the U.S., including Chicago, Seattle, Milwaukee and St. Louis. A few other Irish place name possibilities: Dublin, Ennis, Donegal, Carlow, Tralee and Derry.

Gandy

Irish surname, derivation unknown.

A dandy, bouncy family name with tap shoes, high hat, and cane. There are several theories of its derivation, including as a nickname from the word 'ganty,' for a person who commonly wore gloves, or from 'gamen,' for someone good at games.

Gandy dancer is a slang term for the early railroad workers who laid and maintain tracks, and it's often heard in old railroad songs.

Gardener

English, "keeper of the garden"

Gardener is surely one of the most pleasant and evocative of the occupational options, calling up images of green grass and budding blooms. The name can also be spelled without the first '*e*', as in Gardner (born George Cadogan Gardner) McCay, a hunky TV heartthrob of the 1950s and 60s. Gardner is a much more common surname spelling, associated with screen legend Ava, mystery writer Erle Stanley and art collector and patron Isabella Stewart, founder of Boston's Gardner Museum.

Gareth

Welsh, "gentle"

Gareth, the name of a modest and brave knight in King Arthur's court, makes a sensitive, gently appealing choice, used more in its native Wales than anywhere else.

The name Gareth first appeared in Malory's *Morte d'Arthur*, as the lover of Eluned, the brother of Gawain and nephew of King Arthur. He also appears in the Gareth and Lynette segment of Tennyson's *Idylls of the King*. In the British version of *The Office*, Gareth is the name of the equivalent character of Dwight Schrute, and it also appeared in *Four Weddings and a Funeral*. Recommended nickname: Gaz. Not recommended nickname: Gary.

Gatsby

German surname and literary name

Suddenly, we're hearing the name Gatsby, as in *The Great* character by F. Scott Fitzgerald, used as a first name for girls as well as boys. The book's Jay Gatsby gussied up his name from Gatz, whose meaning is given variously as left-handed, cat, God, and person from Gat. As a first name, it's got a lot of energy and that great pedigree.

Giacomo

ZHAHK — oh-moh

Italian variation of James, "supplanter"

Giacomo is a primo member of the Giovanni-Giancarlo-Gianni-Giacomo gruppo of Italian names that are beginning to be adopted by American parents. Singer/creative baby namer Sting chose it for his son.

Giacomo has many notable native namesakes, including composer Puccini, lothario Casanova and poet Leopardi.

Gower

Welsh, "pure"

This Old Welsh name associated with blacksmiths has never caught on, but it has the right two-syllable occupational feel to qualify for revival. Gower Champion was a successful midcentury dancer, choreographer and director on the Broadway stage, in films and on TV.

Granger

English occupational name, "worker of the granary"

If you're seeking a solid last-name-first occupational name with a warm, friendly sound, one that's not overused, this could be it.

Granger is much better known as a surname — think handsome mid-century actors Stewart and Farley, and, more recently and majorly, Hermione Jean Granger, one of the three main protagonists of the *Harry Potter* series — but would make an unusual but accessible first.

Grey

Color name

The girls have Violet and Scarlet and Ruby and Rose, but for the boys there's a much more limited palette of color names. Grey/Gray is one exception, which could make for a soft and evocative — if slightly somber — choice, especially in the middle. Kaitlin Olson and Rob McElhenney named their son Leo Grey.

A common surname, Grey/Gray is still an unusual first name choice, while longer forms Grayson and Greyson are climbing rapidly, with Grayson at Number 97 and his twin at 200.

The best known bearer of the name, former Governor Gray Davis of California, was born Joseph Graham Davis, Jr, and others with Grey/Gray names include Graydon Carter, editor of *Vanity Fair*, and Grayer, the child in *The Nanny Diaries*.

Gulliver

Irish, "glutton"

Gulliver is an obscure Gaelic surname known almost solely through its literary *Travels* until actor Gary Oldman used it for his son, instantly transforming it into a lively option. British actors Damian Lewis, of *Homeland*, and Helen McCrory also have a son named Gulliver.

Gunther

German, "bold warrior"

When it's spelled with two dots over the '*u*' in German, Gunther is pronounced GUWN-ter, but it has a much softer sound when the 'h' is voiced by English-speakers, as it was, for example, for the name of a character in *Friends*.

Gunther has never been as well used in this country as the Scandinavian version, Gunnar, which now ranks at Number 502, making Gunther all the more distinctive.

Well-known Gunthers include German novelist Gunt(h)er Grass and the character in the German epic poem *Die Nibelungenlied*, which formed the basis for Richard Wagner's Ring cycle of operas.

H

Hallam

English surname, "at the rocks"

A relatively rare English place and surname, Hallam could make a distinctive but usable boy's name. Hallam was the surname of the beloved Cambridge friend whose death Alfred, Lord Tennyson, mourns in his famous poem *In Memoriam. A.H.H.* Tennyson's eldest son, whom he named Hallam, became a Governor-General of Australia.

There was a silent screen actor named Hallam Cooley, and a 2007 Scottish film titled *Hallam Foe*, with Jamie Bell playing the lead character.

Hamish

HAY-mish

Scottish variation of James, "supplanter"

Just as Seamus/Seumus is Irish for James, Hamish is the Scottish form — one that's not often used here, but still redolent of Olde Scotland. If you're ready to go further than Duncan and Malcolm, out to Laird and Ewan territory, this may be worth consideration. It also sounds just like the Yiddish word for homey.

In Scotland, where it became popular in the second half of the nineteenth century, Hamish is a nickname for a Highlander, and it's a high-ranking name in South Australia, where it's currently in the Top 50.

Some people may have become familiar with Hamish via one of the grooms in *Four Weddings and a Funeral.*

Hendrix

Dutch and German, from first name Hendrik

Hendrix is one of those hip rock and roll names, like Lennon, Jagger and Presley, that have been used by fellow celebs and others, to honor the seminal guitarist/singer/songwriter Jimi. And this one has the trendy 'x' ending, as well.

Hiro

Japanese, "broad, widespread"

Hiro was an apt name for a hero of the show *Heroes* — and for our times. Widely used in Japan, sometimes also for girls. Hiroshi is a long form.

Hopper

English, "leaper, dancer"; Dutch, "hop grower or seller"

Sean and Robin Wright Penn chose this name for their son to honor their friend Dennis Hopper; others might associate it with the painter Edward. Couldn't be more spirited.

Huck

Diminutive of Huckleberry, word name

Though forever tied to Huck, short for Huckleberry, Finn, this is an undeniably cute short form that may have some life as part of the hipster taste for names like Duke and Bix.

Huxley

English, "inhospitable place"

Huxley is definitely rising as a surname name, with its *X* that makes almost any name cooler.

Huxley honors writer Aldous, author of *Brave New World*, and other members of his distinguished family — and nickname Hux is nearly as adorable as Huck.

I

Ilario

ee-LAH-ree-o

Latin from Greek, "cheerful, happy"

Ilario's merry, jovial sound reflects a shared root with the word hilarious.

Indio

Spanish, "Indian"

This name of a California desert town, used by Deborah Falconer and Robert Downey, Jr. for their son, makes a much livelier and more individual — not to mention more masculine — improvisation on the themes of India and Indiana.

The similar sounding color name Indigo is unisex, but tending more to the girls — it was used by Lou Diamond Phillips for his daughter, as well as the group The Indigo Girls, but its *o*-ending makes it boy-friendly too.

Inigo

Basque, medieval Spanish variation of Ignatius, "fiery"

Inigo, almost unknown in the U.S., is an intriguing choice, with its strong beat, creative and evocative sound, and associations with the great early British architect and stage designer Inigo Jones. The sixteenth-seventeenth century Jones shared his name with his father, a London clockmaker, who received it when Spanish names were fashionable in England, especially among devout Roman Catholics.

Inigo Montoya is a major character in *The Princess Bride*, played by Mandy Patinkin.

The pronunciation is with short i's and a hard g: IN-ih-go.

Italo

Italian, "from Italy"

You can't get more Italian than this name of the daddy of legendary twins Romulus and Remus, founders of Rome. A noted bearer is acclaimed Italian journalist and novel and short story writer Italo Calvino, author of *Invisible Cities* and *If on a winter's night a traveler.*" Trivia tidbit: Calvino was actually one of his middle names.

Ivar

EE-v ahr

Norse, "yew wood, archer"

Part of a small group of similar names with similar roots — Ivor, Iver, Ivo, Ives — which are all worth looking at. Used throughout Scandinavia, Ivar is currently a Top 100 name in Sweden. In the Willa Cather novel *O Pioneers!*, there is a character known as — oops — Crazy Ivar.

Ivo

German, "yew wood, archer"

Ivo is an unusual, catchy name with the energetic impact of all names ending in '*o*'. Hardly heard in the U.S., it is used a bit more frequently in England, as is the related Ivor, a favorite of such novelists as Evelyn Waugh and P.G. Wodehouse. Ivo is currently most popular in the Netherlands.

J

Janus

Greek, "gateway"

The meaning of this ancient Roman god's name relates to transitions, hence its connection to the name of the first month of the new year, a time of fresh beginnings. Janus is usually depicted as a two-faced god facing in opposite directions, since he looks both to the future and the past. The Slavic form Janusz is more commonly used than the English, represented by the Polish cinematographer Janusz Kaminski, who has shot all of Steven Spielberg's films from *Schindler's List* to *Lincoln*.

But with January having been taken over by the girls, why not consider Janus? One caveat: it does sound a lot like the female Janice.

Japheth

JAY-feth

Hebrew, "expansion"

This name of a son of Noah, whose descendants were said to have populated Europe, was well used by the seventeenth century Pilgrims, but pronunciation challenges hinder its chances for resurgence today.

Japheth is a major character in the Madeleine L'Engle novel *Many Waters*.

Jebediah

Hebrew, "beloved friend"

Like its better known cousin Jedidiah, Jebediah is one of those four-syllable Old Testament names that is being shorn of its long white-bearded image, with the help of its modern-sounding Jeb nickname.

Pop culture references: The Australian alternate rock band Jebediah, and the founder of the Simpson's hometown, Jebediah Springfield.

Jeb Bush, by the way, was not born Jebediah: J.E.B. are his initials, as in John Ellis Bush.

Joab

Hebrew, "praise Jehovah"

Joab is the iblical name of an advisor of David, who led many military victories, and is surely much more usable than the burdened Job. A similar option is Joah, a possible replacement for Jonah or Noah.

Joachim

jo-AE-kim or jo-AH-kum

Hebrew, "Established by God"

Joachim is an undiscovered biblical name with potential, although most modern parents would probably prefer the more lively Spanish version, Joaquin. Like many Old Testament names, it was primarily in use in the seventeenth century, and then became rare. In the Bible Joachim is a king of Judah.

Jonty

Diminutive of Jonathan, "gift of Jehovah"

Jaunty, to say the least, Jonty might be an option if Johnny feels too old school. It has been noticed most often on the playing fields, as in UK rugby player Jonty Parkin (born Jonathan) and South African cricketer Jonty Rhodes (Jonathon).

Joost

yoost

Dutch, "just"

Like many Dutch names, this one, pronounced 'yoost' has an upbeat sound. Also spelled Joos, as in sixteenth century Netherlandish master Joos van Cleve, one of the first to introduce background landscapes in his paintings.

Jorah

Hebrew, "early rain"

Jorah, a Biblical name with a lovely nature-related meaning, might make a fresher alternative to the overused Jordan. It's similar to the feminine Nora, Cora, and Laura, but depending on your viewpoint, that may be an advantage.

Joss

English diminutive of Jocelin, "the merry one"

Joss hadn't been heard much in this country before the emergence of Joss (born Joseph) Whedon, creator of *Buffy the Vampire Slayer, Angel*, et al; it would make a catchy middle name choice. Female British singer Joss Stone was born Jocelyn.

Jotham

Hebrew, "the Lord is perfect"

Jotham is an Old Testament name that today would certainly be the only one in his class, having something of an urban feel via its similarity to the word 'gotham'. In the Bible one Jotham is the sole surviving son of Gideon after the massacre of his brothers, the other is a king of Judah who was an enthusiastic builder. Jotham Riddle is a character in James Fenimore Cooper's novel *The Pioneers*, while Jotham Powell appears in Edith Wharton's *Ethan Frome*.

Jubal

Latin, "joyous celebration"; Hebrew, "ram's horn"

This unusual name might be a possibility for musical families: Jubal was credited in Genesis with the invention of the lyre, flute, harp, and organ. It also has a jubilant feel through its sound and meaning, and has had some southern popularity via Confederate general Jubal Anderson Early. George Eliot wrote a poem called *The Legend of Jubal*.

There have been a few Jubals in contemporary culture as well: Jubal Harshaw in Robert A. Heinlein's sci-fi classic *Stranger in a Strange Land* and Jubal Early in Joss Whedon's TV cult favorite, *Firefly*.

Jupiter

Roman mythology name

Jupiter's partner Juno has entered the mainstream, so it's possible that her divine mate could follow. The name of the supreme Roman deity and the largest planet has until recently had either too hippie or too grandiose a feel for most mortals, but with the rise of sound-alike Juniper and space names such as Orion and Mars, Jupiter may find new favor.

Short form Jupe is adorable.

K

Keats

English literary name, "kite"

Poetic and easier to pronounce (it's keets) than Yeats (which is yates). This one of many poets' names to consider, such as Auden, Eliot, Frost, Byron, Lorca, Marlowe, Blake, Emerson and Tennyson, which was used by Russell Crowe.

Keefe

Irish, "handsome and noble"

Keefe is an energetic Irish surname occasionally used as a first. Only caveat: Will people think your little Keefe is a Keith with enunciation problems?

Keen

Word name

Actor Mark Ruffalo honed this surname down to its basics when he chose it for his son. A more usable expansion might be the Irish surname Keenan/Keenen.

Kelso

Scottish place and surname

This name of a town in Scotland, one of the earliest recorded surnames in the whole British Isles, has more vitality, and is more boyish, than the feminized Kelsey.

Some will surely associate it with the character of Michael Kelso, usually referred to simply as Kelso by his friends, portrayed by Ashton Kutcher on *That '70s Show*.

Kenzo

Japanese, "strong and healthy"

Kenzo is a common Japanese name with several creative bearers: the single-named fashion designer, prizewinning architect Kenzo Takada, and painter Kenzo Okada, which makes it internationally recognizable.

Kenzo was chosen for their son by Kimora Lee Simmons and Djimon Hounsou, inspired by the designer.

Kenzo can have other meanings, all positive, depending on the Japanese characters used.

Kerouac

Breton literary name

Kerouac could make for a meaningful possible modern literary inspiration, via *On the Road* author Jack. The writer's baptism certificate read Jean Louis Kirouac, though he later claimed his full name was Jean-Louis Lebris de Kerouac.

Keverne

Cornish saint and place-name

St. Keverne is a town on Cornwall's Lizard Peninsula and also the name of an ancient saint. While the name is virtually unused for children in the modern world, it could be a Kevin update and has contemporary possibilities.

Kiernan

Irish, "little dark one"

Although this surname name is closely related to the more common Irish name Kieran, Kiernan is also a well used family name, tied to thirty-three ancient chieftains. It has on a few occasions been used for girls.

L

Lachlan

LOCK-lin

Scottish, "from the fjord-land"

Lachlan is as Scottish as haggis and tartan plaid kilts, a favorite used throughout England, Scotland, Australia and New Zealand — and just beginning to be noticed in the US. An ancient name, Lachlan was originally used to describe the Viking invaders of Scotland, those from the land of the lochs.

In Ireland, the name was Anglicized as Laughlin; in Scotland the pet forms are Lach, Lachie or Lockie.

Lachlan has been a top name in Australia for at least a decade and is currently Number 3 there. It has been in the headlines recently via the eldest son of media mogul Rupert Murdoch.

Somewhat surprisingly, Lachlan has US presidential cred, as the son of tenth president John Tyler, whose other children included a Lyon, a Letitia, a Tazewell and a Pearl.

Laird

Scottish, "lord of the land"

Laird is a Scottish title for the landed gentry -it ranks just below a Baron — with a pleasantly distinctive Scottish burr that must have appealed to Sharon Stone, who chose it for her son.

Laird Cregar was an early movie actor, known for playing creepy roles; Laird Hamilton is a famous American big-wave surfer.

Lancelot

French, "servant"

In Arthurian legend, Lancelot was one of the most dashing of the Knights of the Round Table who eventually had an affair with Queen Guinevere: it makes for a romantic story — but perhaps overly romantic — name.

An older spelling is Launcelot, as seen in Shakespeare's Launcelot Gabbo in *The Merchant of Venice* and two Tobias Smollett novels.

Short form Lance has had an independent life of his own.

Land

Word name or diminutive of Landon, "long hill"
One of the simplest, most down-to-earth yet evocative of the word names, which could work — especially as a middle.

Langston

English, "tall man's town"
The great African-American Harlem Renaissance writer Langston Hughes put this one on the map; actor Laurence Fishburne adopted it for his now grown son, born in 1987.

Hughes was born James Mercer Langston Hughes, Langston being his mother's maiden name.

Some similar choices are Lanford, Landon, Langford and Langley.

Laszlo

LAZ-lo

Hungarian, "glorious ruler"
The Hungarian classic Laszlo, with its zippy 'z' middle and energetic 'o' ending, has become something of a hipster option, beginning to be considered by cutting-edge parents.

A name with a royal heritage in its native country in the Ladislaus form, it is still in the Hungarian Top 20.

Laszlo is probably most familiar to Americans via the noble Paul Henreid character in *Casablanca*, who was Czech; there have been other fictional Laszlos in *Real Genius* and the *Doctor Who* series, and Laszlo is the name of the Ralph Fiennes character in *The English Patient*.

Real life namesakes include painter Moholy-Nagy and acclaimed cinematographer Kovacs. Two well-known actors who were born with the name Laszlo are Peter Lorre and Leslie Howard.

The spelling of the name can be streamlined to Lazlo.

Latham

English from Scandinavian, "the barn"

This familiar surname with a surprising meaning could be added to your list of undiscovered 'last names first' names.

Laurent

lor-AHN

French variation of Lawrence, "of Laurentium"

A French accent makes almost everything sound better, especially when attached to a *Twilight* vampire. Laurent also has a high-style feel via designer Yves St-Laurent. Laurent de Brunhoff is the French author-illustrator who continued his father Jean's series of *Babar* books.

Lazarus

Greek variation of Hebrew Eleazar, "God helps"

Lazarus is a name that looks as if it could possibly be raised from the dead, just like its biblical bearer. Look for it in the next wave of Old Testament revivals that transcend their long-bearded images, the way Noah, Moses, and Abraham have for this generation.

In the Bible, there are two people named Lazarus, the better known being the brother of Mary and Martha of Bethany whom Jesus raised from the dead. There have been also several saints named Lazarus.

As a surname, Lazarus is most identified with poet Emma Lazarus, whose words are displayed on the Statue of Liberty.

Related options are the original Hebrew Eleazar, the Italian and Spanish Lazaro, and the Yiddish form Lazer/Laser, the name of the son in the film *The Kids are All Right*.

Lazer

Yiddish variation of Eliezer or Lazarus, "God helps"

Lazer has some biblical cred as a form of Eliezer, Eleazar, or Lazarus, all relatives, and it's also a modern bad boy name a la Ranger and Breaker. Our recommendation would be to use one of the biblical forms as the proper name and Lazer as a nickname.

Leith

Scottish, place name from the Scottish port town
This is an unusual surname of medieval Scottish origin that might serve as a possible alternative to the aging Keith, though it's a bit tough on the tongue. Leith is also an Arabic name meaning 'lion'.

Leonid

Russian, variation of Leonidas, "lion"
This form got noticed as the first name of long-reigning Russian president Brezhnev; other bearers include playwright and short-story writer Andreyev, Leonid the Magnificent, a Russian performance artist on *America's Got Talent,* and Leonid McGill, the protagonist of a Walter Mosley private eye series. All in all, though, Leonid is not the most likely to join the pride of lion-related names here.

Lev

leev

Hebrew, "heart"; Russian and Czech, "lion"
This concise one-syllable form of Leo has definite potential, being more unusual than the increasingly popular Levi.

The leonine Lev is the Russian birth name of the great novelist Tolstoy, and the mother of Liev Schreiber has stated that she named him in honor of the writer. In the Chaim Potok novel *My Name is Asher Lev,* about a Hasidic Jewish boy in New York, Lev is the character's surname.

Actress Candace Cameron has a son she named Lev.

Lior

Hebrew, "I have a light"
Lior is a unisex name frequently heard in Israel, capturing the popular light theme through its meaning. For English speakers, the one down side is possible pronunciation confusion with "liar," though it really rhymes with Eeyore.

Loch

Scottish Gaelic, "lake"
Loch is a watery word that sounds more like a name because it's one step removed from its English form. Pronounced as "lock," it's also a short form of the variously-spelled Lachlan.

Lodge

English, "shelter"

This English surname offers an interesting mix of images: it sounds upper-crusty yet macho, and also conjures up the coziness of a wintery ski lodge. As a surname it is associated with the Massachusetts Republican Senate Minority Leader in the Woodrow Wilson era, Henry Cabot Lodge, who was the father of poet George Cabot Lodge and grandfather of Senator Henry Cabot Lodge, Jr., who was ambassador to the UN and Richard Nixon's 1960 presidential running mate.

Longfellow

English, "tall one"

Longfellow is the first name of the eponymous hero of the classic 1936 film *Mr. Deeds Goes to Town*, later remade with Adam Sandler. But it's hard to imagine a modern parent using it except as a middle name to honor the poet.

Lorcan

Irish, "little, fierce"

Lorcan is a name rich in Irish history as belonging to several kings, including the grandfather of the most famous high king of Ireland, Brian Boru. Lorcan O'Toole, known in English as Laurence O'Toole, is the patron saint of Dublin, so it's not too surprising that Irish-born actor Peter O'Toole named his son Lorcan.

In the *Harry Potter* epic, Lorcan is the twin son of Luna Lovegood Scamander.

Strong, easy to pronounce and spell, Lorcan is an Irish name that would stand out from the more common crop of Connors and Liams.

Lucan

Irish from Latin, "light"

Lucan is a rarely heard Irish name, a Luke form with the trendy an ending.

Ludovic

English and Scottish variation of Ludwig, "famous warrior"

Euro-cool. Heard more in Scotland than in England or the US, Ludovic Lesly is a character in the Sir Walter Scott novel *Quentin Durward* and Sir Ludovic Kennedy was a noted Scottish broadcaster and writer. Cute nickname: Ludo.

M

Maclean

Scottish, "servant of Saint John"

Whether you pronounce it Mac-cleen or Mac-clayn, this is one of the crispest and most appealing of the Mac names. The Scottish clan Maclean is one of the oldest of the Highland Scottish clans. Trivia tidbit: Sir Fitzroy Maclean is said to have been an inspiration for the Ian Fleming James Bond character.

Macon

French place name

What with Mason scooting up the charts, this attractive place-name, with its thick Georgia accent, could make a more distinctive alternative.

Macon has played major roles in two novels, Anne Tyler's *The Accidental Tourist* and Toni Morrison's *Song of Solomon*, in the latter as both a Macon Sr. and Jr.

Madigan

Irish, "little dog"

A jovial and jaunty Irish name, the title of a long-gone TV crime drama, this would make an appealing choice. Slight downside: sharing the nickname Maddy with many little Madelines and Madisons.

Madoc

Welsh, "fortunate, benefactor's son"

Also spelled Madog, which was the name of an early Welshman, Madog ap Owain Gwynedd, reputed to have been the first European to discover North America in 1155. Maddox, the name of Angelina Jolie and Brad Pitt's oldest child, is a stronger and more familiar choice.

Magnus

Latin, "greatest"

Magnus, a powerful name with a commanding presence, is one of the newly unearthed ancient artifacts; it dates back to Charlemagne being called Carolus Magnus, or Charles the Great. It was picked for their sons by Will Ferrell (whose wife Viveca Paulin is Swedish), Kirsty Swanson and Elizabeth Banks.

A royal appellation in Scandinavia, Magnus was the name of six early kings of Norway and four of Sweden; it is still a Top 6 name in Denmark and Norway.

Magnus has made appearances as a vampire in Anne Rice's *Vampire Chronicles* and as a character in Roald Dahl's *Matilda*. And for an extra ego boost, in Charles Dickens's *The Pickwick Papers*, there's the following dialogue: 'Magnus is my name. It's rather a good name, I think, sir.' 'A very good name, indeed," said Mr. Pickwick.

Maguire

Irish, "son of the beige one"

Although Maguire is such a prominent Irish surname — it ranks in the Top 40 in the Emerald Isle — this lively and cheerful family name has rarely been used as a first, unlike more familiar examples like Ryan, Riley and Reagan. The powerful and distinguished Maguire clan was known for their courage, leadership and resilience. The name's many notable associations include the unionizing Pennsylvania coal miners known as the Molly Maguires, actor Tobey Maguire and Dixie Chick Martie Maguire. Other spellings are McGuire and McGwire; two other handsome Irish surnames to consider are Malone and Magee.

Mailer

Occupational name, English or French, "enameler"

Mailer is one of the more unusual of the on-trend occupational surnames. Recommended for fans of the macho writer Norman Mailer.

Malachy

Irish version of Malachi, Hebrew, "my messenger"

This spelling, which came to the attention of readers of the best-selling *Angela's Ashes* as the name of author Frank McCourt's father and brother, the latter of whom wrote a best-seller of his own, lends the biblical name a more expansive, almost boisterous image.

Malachy is also the anglicized version of Melaghlin, one of St. Patrick's first companions. It was borne by the High King Malachy, who defeated the

Vikings at the Battle of Tara in 980. St. Malachy was a reformer who reorganized the church in Ireland after the Viking raids.

Irish actor Cillian Murphy has a son named Malachy.

Manfred

German, "man of peace"

Hipsters might consider reviving this old German name, though we're not so sure their sons wouldn't have preferred the classic Fred name Frederick. Manfred B. Lee (born Manford) was half of the team of detective story writers who used the pseudonym Ellery Queen; Manfred Mann was a British pop group of the 1960's, with Manfred Mann (born Michael Liebowitz) at the keyboard. There's also a wooly mammoth named Manfred, and nicknamed Manny, in the film *Ice Age*.

Mannix

Irish, "a little monk"

An *X*-ending surname less common than the Jolie-Pitt-inspired Maddox. Grandparents might still associate it with the old TV crime show.

Manus

Irish variation of Magnus, "greatest"

This is an old Irish name associated with such heroes as the seventeenth century chieftain, scholar and poet Manus O'Donnell. In this country, though, parents would not find Manus as pleasing or impressive as Magnus.

Maoz

mah-ohz

Hebrew, "fortress, strength"

Maoz is a symbolic name given to boys born at Hannukah because of the song "Maoz Tzur," "Rock of Ages," which is sung at that time.

March

Word name

Along with August, March is one of the few month names available to boys; this brisk single-syllable name might be worth considering as either a first or middle option. As a surname, it brings warm memories of the girls of *Little Women*, and of twentieth century actor Fredric.

Marino

Latin, "of the sea"

Marino is an Italian first and surname with distinct crossover possibilities, having pleasant seaside undertones, and is far more unusual in the U.S. than sister Marina.

Marino Marini was an Italian sculptor who has a museum dedicted to his work in Florence; Dan Marino a record-breaking football quarterback.

Marlow

English, "driftwood"

Marlow is a suave, unusual surname-name that was chosen by Celine designer Phoebe Philo for her older son. Caveat: it sounds just like the feminine Marlo and, with the addition of a final 'e', has begun to be used for girls.

Maro

Latin, Hebrew, or Japanese, "from Mars; bitter; or, myself"

Maro is an ancient saints' name — he was an Italian follower of St. Flavia and was martyred — rarely used in modern life. The name Maro may stem from the Roman Marcellus, related to Mars, the god of war, or it may be a feminine form of Maria, connected with Mario. Maro is also a Japanese name meaning "myself."

And why couldn't Maro be more widely used today? As a masculine spin on stylish Mara, it certainly could.

Mars

Roman mythology god of war

The name of the Roman god of war began to sound less intimidating when Erykah Badu gave it to her daughter, and musicians Thomas and Bruno Mars (the latter born Peter Hernandez) have given it a modern edge. Mars actually could make a pleasant, planetary middle name for either sex.

Massimo

Italian variation of Maximus, "the greatest"

Massimo is a Latin charmer, much more appealing than the old-fashioned Mario, and is a charismatic member of the Maximus/Magnus family.

Mattias

Scandinavian, spelling variation of Matthias, "gift of God"

This particular spelling was chosen by Will Ferrell for his son, brother to Magnus. These names are both popular in Sweden, birthplace of their mother, Viveca Paulin.

Maxfield

English, "Mac's field"

This name may be related to the Latin Maximus, which means "the greatest," or to a British landowner's name, but for most modern parents, it's one of several ways to get to short form Max.

Probably its most noted bearers is influential twentieth century painter and illustrator Maxfield Parrish, who was born Frederick but later adopted the maiden name of his maternal grandmother.

Maxon

Invented elaboration of Max, Latin, "greatest"

The newly-styled Maxon takes its cue from Jaxon, another elaboration of a classic name on the rise. Maxon is not bad, as invented names go, yet it's hard for us to advocate for Maxon over Maxwell, Maxfield, Maximus, or just plain Max.

Mccoy

Irish variation of McKay, "fire"

One of numerous usable Irish and Scottish surnames starting with Mac and Mc, this is the real McCoy. McCoy Tyner, the well-known jazz pianist, is one of the few to use it as a first name, though he was born Alfred McCoy Tyner.

Merce

Diminutive of Mercer, "a merchant"

Merce Cunningham (born with the French version Mercier) was a highly influential avant garde dancer-choreographer and his name still resonates with an aura of bold originality.

Merrick

Anglo-Welsh, "fame, power"

A strong, attractive surname name with a mix of possible origins: either from the Welsh first name Meuric, which is a form of Maurice, and contains Germanic elements meaning fame and power, or from a Scottish Gaelic word meaning a fork in a river or a road, which led to the name of several places named Merrick in Scotland.

Despite its ancient history, Merrick these days sounds more modern than the somewhat tired Derek.

Milos

Slavic, diminutive of Miloslav, "lover of glory"
Commonly heard in Greece as well as the Slavic cultures, Milos has been associated in this country with Czech film director Milos Forman. Pronounced MEE-losh, it's a more original ethnic spin on the popular Miles and Milo.

Mingus

Scottish, variation of Menzies, "tenants of a manor"
Supermodel Helena Christensen named her son in honor of jazz great Charles Mingus, opening up a whole category of jazzy possibilities: Kenton, Calloway, Ellington, Gillespie, Mulligan, Tatum, and Thelonius.

Molloy

Irish, "a venerable chieftain"
There are many dynamic three-syllable Irish surnames; this is one of the rarer two-syllable ones. *Molloy* is the title of a 1951 novel by Samuel Beckett, initially written in French. Another Beckett novel of naming interest is *Malone Dies.*

Moore

English place-name, "the moors"
Moore is recommended as a rich and satisfying middle name choice, whether it relates to your own family history or not. Of the numerous outstanding Moore-surnamed namesakes, count sculptor Henry, writers Clement, Marianne and Brian, entertainers Demi, Dudley, Garry, Roger, Julianne, Melba and Mary Tyler, and provocateur Michael.

Mordecai

Hebrew, from the Persian, "warrior"
Mordecai, although it has a noble heritage, has never caught on in this country, because of its rather weighty image.

Mordecai is a symbolic name for boys born on the holiday of Purim, because this cousin of Queen Esther helped her save the Jews from destruction at the hands of Haman.

Mordecai Richler was a Canadian author and screenwriter whose best known work is *The Apprenticeship of Duddy Kravitz*.

Morrison

English, "son of Morris"

Morrison is one of the more uncommon patronymics; it could be used to honor an ancestral Morris, or one of the well-known surnamed Morrisons: Toni, Jim or Van.

Morrissey

Irish, "descendant of Muiris"

When British rocker Steven Patrick Morrissey decided to use his last name alone, it became a viable option for baby namers, a lot cooler than Morris or Maurice, with the nice three-syllable lilt of of such other Irish surnames as Finnegan and Flanagan. It can also be spelled Morrisey.

Morrison is a related possibility, also with musical ties, to Irish singer-songwriter Van (born George Ivan).

Moss

English, "descendant of Moses"; word name

This evocative green nature name, heard much more frequently as a surname, is associated with playwright Moss Hart (born Robert), who co-wrote (with George S. Kaufman) such enduring Broadway comedies as *The Man Who Came to Dinner* and *You Can't Take it With You*.

Never having made it onto the popularity list, Moss would make a distinctively fresh and attractive alternative to Ross.

Prominent bearers of Moss as a surname include British auto racer Stirling, supermodel Kate, and Elisabeth Moss, best known as Peggy Olson on *Mad Men*.

N

Neo

Latin, "new"

This nouveau name of Keanu Reeves's character in *The Matrix* has not enjoyed the same burst of popularity as its female counterpart, Trinity, but it definitely sounds, well, newer. Neo Rauch is an interesting contemporary German artist.

Neville

French, "new town"

More often used in Britain than here, where most names ending in ville fall into the unthinkable class, this might make an exception via fans of the musical Neville Brothers.

Charles Dickens used the name for a character in his unfinished novel *The Mystery of Edwin Drood*.

Nicholson

English, "son of Nicol"

If you're looking for a Nicholas substitute or namesake, Nicholson would make a more distinctive path to the likable nickname Nick, fitting in with other newer patronymics like Anderson and Harrison. Unusual but not outlandish, it is associated with writer Nicholson Baker, library advocate and author of *Vox*. And as a surname, of course, with Jack.

Nicolo

Italian form of Nicholas, "people of victory"

Nicolo is a more lively and exotic variation of Nicholas. A name with a long, distinguished Italian history of its own, it also boasts the charming nickname Nico.

Although the female counterpart, Nicola, has long been a favorite in the UK, Nicolo has not yet made a similar transition. It was chosen, though, by actor Stanley Tucci, for his son.

Nicolo is a name with musical reverberations, connected to the major early violin maker Amati, and the later violin virtuoso Paganini.

O

O'Brien

Irish,, "descendant of Brian"

The use of O-prefixes could create the next wave of Irish-inflected names, offering an innovative way of honoring a relative with the old-fashioned moniker Brian. On *Downton Abbey*, the surname O'Brien was heard so often, it began to seem like a first.

Oak

Tree name

Oak, a symbol of solidity, strength, and longevity, is joining Cedar and Pine as a viable name, one that would work especially well in the middle.

If you'd prefer to take the longer route to the name, you can consider the surnames Oakes or Oakley.

Obadiah

Hebrew, "servant of God"

For the seriously audacious biblical baby namer who wants to move beyond Elijah and Josiah, this name has considerable old-fangled charm. Obadiah, who gave his name to one of the shortest books in the Bible, was a rich man who had the gift of prophecy. There are several other men named Obadiah in the Bible, as well as a Saint Obadiah.

In literature, there is an Obadiah in Laurence Sterne's novel *Tristan Shandy*, and another in Anthony Trollope's *Barchester Towers*.

Obadias

Variation of Obadiah, Hebrew, "servant of God"

Obadias, with its appealing 's' ending, could be an even fresher way to spin the biblical Obadiah.

Odysseus

Greek mythology name, "wrathful"

The name of the brave, resourceful hero of Homer's epic saga has almost always been considered too weighty for a child to bear, but at this point, some brave, resourceful parents out there might be willing to take it on.

Oisin

oh-SHEEN

Irish, "little deer"

Oisin, also spelled as the phonetic Osheen and still a popular name in Ireland today, was the mythological son of Finn McCool and Sadb, the goddess who was changed into a deer. A legendary war hero and poet, Oisin had a name that is also reminiscent in sound of the ocean. Pronounced correctly, this name has an attractive sheen.

Ossian is another version, reflected in the eighteenth century Ossianic poems of James Macpherson, which transformed him into a Scottish hero and also popularized the names Oscar, Fingal, Selma and Malvina.

Olivier

o-LIV-ee-ay

French, "olive tree"

More and more frequently heard as the Gallic version of Oliver, Olivier could be seen as a tribute to the great British actor, Sir Laurence O.

Onyx

Gem name

Unlike Pearl and Ruby, this is one gem name suited for boys, the final x making it sound strong and virile.

Osgood

Teutonic, "divine creator"

This name seems to foresee a future CFO. Not a bad thing. Osgood Perkins is the name of both the father and son of actor Anthony. Oz is the enlivening nickname.

Oz

Hebrew, "strength, powerful, courageous"

This may be a legitimate Hebrew name denoting power, but to any American kid, it will evoke ruby slippers and a yellow brick road. The full Hebrew name is Ozni, who was a grandson of Jacob in the Bible.

Ozias

Greek, "salvation"

Everyone says they want an unusual name — well, if you truly do, this is one with Biblical cred that fits the bill, with the added attraction of the user-friendly nickname of Ozzie/Ozzy. Ozias is the name of several minor figures in the Bible. Osias is another spelling.

P

Pace

Word name

Calm, straightforward, patrician sounding: Pace is one new-style name that's well grounded.

Painter

Occupational name.

Painter is among the most creative choices in this very fashionable category of names, with a particularly pleasant sound. Whereas most occupational names conjure up physical labor, this one feels like a gateway to the arts.

Actor Chad Lowe used it as the middle name of his daughter Mabel.

Paolo

Italian, variation of Paul, "small"

Paolo is an irresistibly lush name, worlds more romantic than its spare English equivalent.

Among noted bearers of the name are Renaissance painters Uccello and Veronese, architect Soleri, and whole teams of Italian soccer players — or so it seems.

Another possibility is the Spanish version of Paul: Pablo, as in Picasso and Casals.

Pascoe

Cornish variation of Pascal, "Easter"

Pascoe was popular in medieval times and is definitely deserving of revival, especially for a child born in the Easter season. Other spellings are Pasco and Pascow.

Paterson

English, "son of Peter"

Paterson is a surname-name to continue a line of Peters and also the name of a city in New Jersey, hometown of poets William Carlos Williams and Allen Ginsberg.

Pax

Latin, "peaceful"

Pax, one of the variations of names meaning peace that are newly popular in these less-than-peaceful times, got a lot of publicity when chosen by Brad & Angelina for their Vietnamese-born son. Parents attracted to Pax may also want to consider Paz, the unisex Spanish version, or Paxton, a growing-in-popularity surname choice that shares that magical X-factor.

Penn

English, "enclosure"

This simple, elegant name offers something for many kinds of parents, from writers and history buffs to photographers to Pennsylvania dwellers. Most famous bearers are comedian Penn Jillette and *Gossip Girl* hottie Penn Badgley, both of whom were given this distinctive name at birth. Long obscure, Penn seems destined for greater usage.

More familiar as a surname, Penn has had a number of distinguished bearers, including Pennsylvania founder William, director Arthur, photographer Irving, and actor/activist Sean.

Peregrine

Latin, "traveler, pilgrim"

Peregrine is considered to be an elegantly aristocratic name in England, but has never made it to the U.S., where it has been seen as extravagantly eccentric. In the new naming climate, though, it's not beyond consideration — in fact it's already been chosen by at least one Berry.

The meaning of Peregrine, which was borne by several early saints, relates to the transitory nature of life on earth, having nothing to do with the peregrine falcon. In literature, it is best known from the central character of Tobias Smollett's novel *Peregrine Pickle*.

Historically, Peregrine was the name chosen for the first English child born in the New World — actually on the Mayflower when it was docked in Provincetown.

And there's always the *Mad Men*-era nickname Perry to make Peregrine more user-friendly.

Perez

Spanish from Hebrew, "to blossom"

The newest surname names are ethnic rather than Waspy, and this is an excellent example, associated these days with gossip blogger Perez (born Mario) Hilton.

Phelan

FAY-lan

Irish, "wolf"

Phelan, pronounced FAY-lan or FEE-lan, is an appealing Irish surname name, with a rich history in Irish myth and religious and secular life. One bearer was a fiercely loyal follower of the legendary warrior Finn MacCool, another was a missionary saint.

The first name Phelan figures in an O'Henry story, "Between Rounds"; and in *The Help*, Skeeter's surname is Phelan. In Irish, the name is spelled Faolan.

Phineas

Hebrew, "oracle"

Julia Roberts drew the biblical Phineas into the limelight when she chose it, with the even-more-antique spelling Phinnaeus, for her twin son, now called Finn. Phineas had last been heard from via circus impresario Phineas T. Barnum, until it was brought somewhat up to date via the Disney Channel animated show *Phineas and Ferb*.

Anthony Trollope combined name and nickname for the young, handsome and charming Irish lawyer hero of his eponymous novel, *Phineas Finn*. Phineas is also the name of three biblical personages and was popular among the seventeenth century Puritans. Jazz pianist Phineas Newborn, Jr. is a contemporary namesake.

Trivia note: In early movies, characters named Phineas had nicknames like Prune, Whipsnake and Whoopee.

Bottom line: A quirky path to nickname Finn.

Piero

Italian, variation of Peter, "rock"

Piero is elegant, melodic, appealing. Just picture the muted frescoes of Renaissance artist Piero della Francesca.

Piers

Greek, "rock"

Piers was the first version of Peter to reach the English-speaking world, via the Normans, but it's never made it in the US, despite its large measure of understated panache. This might change due to the high visibility of TV personality and former news editor Piers Morgan.

There's a famous satirical medieval poem called *Piers Plowman*, in which the title character symbolizes the virtues of honesty and industry. Piers Whiteoak is a main character in the sixteen-book series *Jalna* by Canadian author Mazo de la Roche; Piers Polkiss is the best friend of Harry's cousin Dudley in the *Harry Potter* books.

The surname form of the name, Pierce, is better known in the U.S., partly via actor Pierce Brosnan.

Piet

Peet

Dutch, diminutive of Pieter, "rock"

Wonderful nickname name most often associated in this country with Dutch modernist painter Mondrian. Pronounced PEET.

Pike

Animal name, "pike, a fish"

The field of nature names is constantly expanding to include all species of flowers and trees and animals and birds — and even fish. In addition to its appeal for anglers, Pike recalls Zebulon Pike, the explorer who discovered and gave his name to Pike's Peak.

While Pike also shares the friendly feel of names like Mike and Ike, the word pike can also be a noun or verb referring to a long sharp weapon used to do not-very-friendly things to people.

Piran

Irish, "prayer"

It may be a longshot, but Piran could conceivably be a future Kieran, which is shaping up to being the next Conor. Piran is the patron saint of miners.

Pitney

English, "island, dry ground in moss"

A name you would probably want to use only if it's in your family history. The first syllable moves it miles away from the softer Whitney.

Pitt

English, "pit, ditch"

Despite two distinguished surname-bearers — the great British statesman William Pitt and heartthrob Brad, this would be a tough name to pull off in first place. William Thackeray used it for two generations of baronets in his novel *Vanity Fair*, the Sir Pitt Crawleys.

Placido

Italian and Spanish, "serene"

Opera star Domingo was responsible for giving this popular Latin name its green card. It was commonly used by early Christians to convey their serenity in the faith, and it was borne by several minor saints.

Plaxico

Latin, "peaceful"

Pittsburgh Steelers wide receiver Plaxico Burress brought this name, which was inherited from an uncle, into the mix, adding to the category of names with peaceful meanings.

Poe

English, "peacock"

An evocative unisex one-syllable name, Poe is most distinguished by its literary reference. Edgar Allan Poe was an influential American author and poet, credited with inventing the genres of detective and science fiction, which might provide inspiration for parents who are fans.

The female singer-songwriter professionally known as Poe was born with the more prosaic name Ann.

The variant spelling Po is identified with Po Bronson, the chronicler of the technological age, and also has the geographical association with the river in northern Italy.

Pom

French diminutive, "apple"

Pom is a shortened word name that's not much used in France, but cute and familiar here as one of Babar (the Elephant's) triplets. Pom, pommy and pommie are (non-derogatory) terms sometimes used by Australians, New Zealanders and South Africans to denote a person of English heritage.

Prescott

English, "priest's cottage"

Prescott is one of several distinguished, upper-crusty surnames beginning with P.

There are several historical surnamed Prescotts, incuding William, a Massachusetts Minuteman and commander at the battle of Bunker Hill, and Samuel, a Revolutonary patriot who traveled with Paul Revere on the night of his famous ride. Prescott is also the first name of the father and brother of George H.W. Bush.

Ptolemy

Greek, "aggressive, warlike"

Pronounced "TAHL-a-mee," this was the name of one of Alexander the Great's generals and several Greco-Egyptian rulers, as well as the name of a famous Greek astronomer. Actress Gretchen Mol brought it into modern times when she chose it for her baby.

Q

Quade

Latin, "fourth" or "born fourth"

Quade is a confident, contemporary-sounding name that would fit right in with classmates Cade, Zade, Slade and Jade, boasting the quirky Q-beginning.

Quade Cooper is an Australian rugby star. With the alternate spelling Quaid, the name is associated with thespian brothers Dennis and Randy.

Quinto

KEEN-toh

Spanish variation of Quintin, "fifth"

Quint or Quinton played to a Latin rhythm.

Quintus

Latin, "fifth"

A literary name figuring in the story of *Ben Hur* and the novels of Anthony Trollope that has the feel of Roman antiquity that is beginning to appeal to many parents. Quintus was one of only about twenty male first names in ancient Rome.

R

Rafferty

Irish, "floodtide, abundance, prosperity"

Jaunty and raffish, Rafferty is one of the most engaging of the Irish surnames, used by Jude Law and Sadie Frost for their son. Fortunately, it doesn't still go by its original form: O'Raighbheartaigh.

Raff and Rafe are two equally great nicknames.

Ranger

French, "forest guardian"

The list of occupational boys' names continues to expand, and this is one of the latest to ride onto the range. And, as trends collide, it also has the popular western, cowboyish feel. A much better choice than the increasingly (and scarily) heard Danger.

Rashid

Arabic, "righteous, rightly advised"

This is a widely used Arabic choice — but Rashad is more popular here. Actress Rashida Jones represents the feminine version.

Reeve

English occupational name, "bailiff"

Reeve is cool and dignified, sophisticated and modern — an excellent combination of assets, and a name being seen as a more masculine and distinctive alternative to Reese.

A reeve was a medieval English manor officer responsible for overseeing the discharge of feudal obligations. Reeve has very occasionally been used for girls: it was the name of the daughter of Charles and Anne Morrow Lindbergh, their youngest child.

Rem

Dutch, diminutive of Remment, Remmert, or Remmelt

The Dutch are fond of short nickname names, and this one is tied to influential and provocative architect Koolhaas, born Remment. Could also be short for Remington or Remy.

Rider

English, "horseman"

Rider is a rock-and-roll baby name, in every sense of the term, though usually spelled Ryder, as in the sons of Kate Hudson and John Leguizamo.

Rio

Spanish, "river"; Brazilian place-name

Rio is a reductive ranchero place-name with an attractive Tex-Mex lilt. No Doubt's Tom Dumont has a son named Rio Atticus.

Also a South American place name, and associated with the Rio Grande, it's been used as a swaggering cowboy name in films spanning from a William S. Hart character in 1915 to Marlon Brando's in *One-Eyed Jacks*. It is occasionally used for a girl, as in the catchy Duran Duran song.

Roald

RO-ahl

Norwegian, "famous ruler"

This intriguing Scandinavian name is associated with Roald Dahl, author of the juvenile classics *James and the Giant Peach* and *Charlie and the Chocolate Factory*. You can honor an ancestral Ronald just by dropping that middle '*n*'.

Robinson

English, "son of Robin"

This can be a cool and unusual way to honor your family Robert, conjuring up memories of *Robinson Crusoe* and *Swiss Family Robinson*, as well as narrative poet Robinson Jeffers, born John Robinson, who shared his mother's middle name.

Rockwell

English, "rock spring"

This would be an intriguing choice for an illustrator's child, thanks to Norman Rockwell and Rockwell Kent.

Rogan

Irish, "redhead"

Rogan makes a great, roguish alternative for the more popular Logan, Ronan and Rowan.

Rohmer

German surname, "pilgrim; fame"

Related to other stylish choices from Roman to Romy to Romeo, Rohmer is a German surname that relates to both Roman pilgrims and the root word for fame. Jennifer Jason Leigh and Noah Baumbach chose this version for their son. The couple's film *Margot at the Wedding* was an homage to French New Wave director Eric Rohmer, who died a few month's before Rohmer Baumbach's birth.

Romulus

Latin, "citizen of Rome"

He was the original Roman, Remus's twin and a founder of Rome. But parents attracted to this name are advised to read the legend first. Romulus does have some less than savory characteristics, including killing his twin brother and making Rome in his own image, and is later deified as Quinnius. Romy and Quinn might make good twin names.

Roone

Irish, "red-haired"

Roone is a lively, attractive and unusual redhead entry brought into the mix by the late TV sports and news executive Roone Arledge, who seemed to own it as a one-person name when he was alive.

Roone can also be seen/used as a short form of Rooney.

Runyon

Irish, "son of a champion"

Runyon is an Irish surname with considerable flair; some will connect it with *Guys and Dolls* writer Damon Runyon.

S

Sailor

Occupational word name

Although this was used by model Christie Brinkley for her daughter, it would be as or even more appropriate for a boy.

Salem

Hebrew and Arabic, "peace"

Salem is a biblical place name in Canaan, as well as that Massachusetts town with its witch-trial associations. But it does have a peaceful meaning and pleasing sound.

Salinger

French, Saint Léger

Fervent fans of *The Catcher in the Rye* might want to consider this as a literary tribute. More mainstream alternative: Holden.

Salman

Arabic, "safety"

Salman is an Arabic name dating back to Salman the Persian, one of Muhammad's companions. In this country it is strongly associated with Anglo-Indian novelist Salman Rushdie, author of *The Satanic Verses*.

Somewhat related names are Salmon, associated with Salmom P. Chase, US Treasury Secretary under Lincoln and the sixth Chief Justice of the Supreme Court; and Zalman, a Yiddish variation of Solomon.

Samar

Arabic, "evening conversation"

This attractive Arabic name is gaining attention in the US, used equally for boys and girls. Indeed, its sound (it rhymes with the feminine Tamar but ends with the fashionably masculine -ar sound as in Oscar) and most logical nickname (Sam) make it a choice that's at once accessible and exotic for both genders.

Sander

Dutch and Scandinavian, diminutive of Alexander, "defending men"
Sander is a more conventional form of Zander or Xander, heard frequently on its own in Europe. It is now a Top 20 name in Norway, and is also popular in Denmark, Belgium and the Netherlands.

Sargent

Spelling variation of Sergeant, Latin, "to serve"
One of the few military ranks used as a name, as in Kennedy in-law and Peace Corps creator Sargent (born Robert Sargent) Shriver. There's also a more creative, artistic association with painter John Singer Sargent.

Sasha

Russian, diminutive of Alexander, "defending men"
The energetic Russian nickname name Sasha is being used increasingly on its own, though somewhat more for girls, especially since the prominence of the First Daughter. Sacha Baron Cohen bears one of the alternate spellings.

Satchel

American nickname
First Woody Allen, then Spike Lee named their children to honor the great early black pitcher, Leroy "Satchel" Paige. A bit luggage-related for non-celebrity use, however.

Sayer

Welsh, "carpenter"
One of the more subtle occupational surnames, Sayer is a pleasant, open, last-name-first name, particularly apt for a family of woodworkers — or writers. Some parents are beginning to consider Sayer as a less popular alternative to Sawyer.

The most well known surnamed Sayer is the British singer Leo Sayer.

Scorpio

Latin, "scorpion"; zodiacal constellation
Of all the astrological names — think Leo, Aries, Gemini — Scorpio probably has the most dramatically potent presence, which could prove something of a burden to a young boy.

In the soap opera *General Hospital*, Scorpio was the character's last name.

Seaton

Scottish and English, "town by the sea"

A perfectly fine Anglo surname, though we'd prefer Keaton. Oscar-winning writer-director George Seaton (*Miracle on 34th Street, The Country Girl*) was actually born George Stenius.

Septimus

Latin, "the seventh son"

Septimus is one of the more dashing of the birth-order Latin number names that were revived by the Victorians. So even if you don't anticipate son number 7, you might be bold enough to consider this relic, certainly preferable to sixth-son name Sextus.

Septimus was popularized by the Roman Emperor Septimus Severus, a patron of arts and letters. There was a Septimus in Wilkie Collins's *The Moonstone*, in Dickens's *The Mystery of Edwin Drood*, and in Trollope's *Barchester* novels. Probably it is most familiar to modern readers as one of the principal characters in Virginia Woolf's *Mrs. Dalloway*, and as *Harry Potter* wizard, Septimus Weasley. There is also *Septimus Heap*, a series of bestselling fantasy novels by Angie Sage.

Severin

French variation of Severus; Latin, "stern, serious"

Severin is an ancient Roman family name borne by several early saints. It's still alive throughout Europe, and could be ready for import here. Severin Winter is a wrestling prodigy character in John Irving's *The 158-Pound Marriage* and, in its original Latin form, Severus Snape appears in *Harry Potter*.

Shaw

English, "dweller by the wood"

With the current taste for last names first, this sounds a lot cooler than Shawn; it also has creative connections to the great Irish playwright, George Bernard Shaw, novelist Irwin Shaw, and Big Band Era clarinetist/bandleader and one-time Ava Gardner husband Artie Shaw.

Since Shaw, like all the other names in this book, has never appeared in the Top 1000, a boy given this name could really make it his own.

Sky

Nature name

Sky is an ambigender nature name that was first legitimized as the character of Sky Masterson in the 1950 musical *Guys and Dolls*, played in the film version by Marlon Brando. It's a name we appreciate for its clear, wide-open feel, less hippyish than others like Rainbow and Starlight, and makes an appealing middle name possibility.

Sky is the name of Sophie's fiancé in *Mamma Mia*, and there are both Power Rangers and Transformers with the name. Elizabeth Berkley used it for her son.

It is also spelled Skye, as in the island in the Inner Hebrides of Scotland. Plus, it's a logical nickname for the variously spelled Schuylers and Skylers.

Slater

English occupational name, "maker of slates"

Slater has a more genial, friendly feel than most trade names. Angela Bassett and Courtney B. Vance used it for one of their twins.

On the nineties TV show *Saved by the Bell*, the character A.C. Slater, played by Mario Lopez, was usually referred to by his surname. Christian Slater is a well-known real life bearer — though he was born Christian Hawkins.

Sören

Danish and Norwegian variation of Severus, "stern"

This gentle Danish name, soft and sensitive, still has more masculine punch than the dated Loren. It's most closely identified with the nineteenth century philosopher Soren Kierkegaard, but there have been modern fictional Sorens as well, in *The Matrix Reloaded* and the book series *Guardians of Ga'Hook, Charlie and Lola*, and *Underworld*.

Sorrel

Botanical name and French, "reddish brown"

Sorrel is a gentle, amber-hued herbal and autumnal name that's used most often to describe the color of a horse. Sorrell is a variant spelling.

Spruce

Tree name

A handsome, spruced-up post-Bruce tree name.

Stanislav

German, Slavic, "someone who achieves glory or fame"

A long-haired classical conductor name, which could appeal to parents looking for a Laszlo-like appellation. This is an old and common name with many spelling variations. Stanislaw Lem was a noted Polish science fiction writer and philosopher, Stanislav Ianevski is the Bulgarian actor who played Viktor Krum in *Harry Potter.*

Stavros

Greek, "cross"

A name that conjures up billionaire shipping magnates like, for instance, Stavros Niarcos.

Steel

Word name

Hard and shiny, Steel projects an image that's smooth, macho...and cold to the touch.

Stefano

Italian variation of Stephen, "garland, crown"

As commonly heard in Rome, Italy as Steve is in Rome, New York. With the accent on the first syllable, Stefano has a lot of seductive charm.

Stellan

Swedish, meaning unknown , possibly "calm"

Stellan is a strong, attractive, Scandinavian possible up-and-comer, known through actor Stellan Skarsgard, and his namesake, the son of Jennifer Connelly and Paul Bettany. Its trendy 'an' ending and the similarity in sound to the popular Kellen/Kellan make it all the more accessible.

Story

Word name

A new unisex word name with a lot of charm, especially appropriate for the child of writers. Jenna Elfman called her son Story Elias.

Stowe

Place-name or surname, "meeting place"

Stowe, the name of a beautiful mountain town in Vermont as well as the surname of the great author Harriet Beecher, is one of the oldest last names on record. The meeting place the name Stowe refers to is part of a church. Stowe might make a distinctive and meaningful middle name for skiers or *Uncle Tom's Cabin* fans.

Sully

French, "stain"; English, "from the south meadow"

A jaunty offshoot of Sullivan, Sully will be associated by kids with the beloved character in the Pixar animated film *Monsters, Inc.* Some notable real-life namesakes are French poet and essayist Sully Prudhomme, the heroic pilot "Sully" Sullenberger, and Sully Erna, lead vocalist of Godsmack.

Sven

Norse, "youth"

Especially for parents of Scandinavian descent, Sven is an accessible and attractive name with an appealing mix of strength and swagger. It comes from the ancient Swedish tribe, the Sviars, who gave their name to Svealand, which later morphed into Sweden.

Sven is now most popular not in its native Sweden but in The Netherlands, where it is currently in the Top 20.

An internationally noted bearer is Swedish cinematographer Sven Nykvist, known for his work on Ingmar Bergman films. Svens have appeared as characters in *Titanic*, Pixar's *Cars* (voiced by Arnold Schwarzenegger), as a Nintendo Pokemon and a manga character, and Marlon Brando portrayed an unlikely Sven in one of his late movies, *Free Money*.

Sweeney

Irish, "the little hero"

The double 'e' gives this Celtic surname a genial sound. It derives from an old Irish name — Suibhne (SHEEV-ne) that was borne by several early saints and kings, including, unfortunately, one known as Mad Sweeney who spent his life living in trees and composing nature poetry. Another possible drawback is the association with Sweeney Todd, the bloodthirsty butcher of Sondheim stage-musical fame.

But if you can put all that aside, Sweeney makes a cheery choice.

Swithun

English, "quick, strong"

Variously spelled Swithun or Swithin, and associated with St. Swithin's day, July 15th, which is famous as a weather predictor a la Groundhog's Day: supposedly, the weather on his feast day will continue for forty days. This would certainly make a unique choice.

T

Tabor

TAY-bor

Hebrew, "a height"; Hungarian, "encampment"

A common name in Hungary, Tabor would stand out here. In the Bible, Tabor is the name of the mountain that stood on the border between northern and southern Israel.

Taddeo

Italian variation of Thaddeus, "gift of God"

A particularly charming spin on the original, as is the Spanish Tadeo.

Tancredo

ton-CRAY-doh

Italian from German, "thoughtful counsel"

A name rich in historic, poetic, and operatic allusions, and an interesting Italian alternative to the more ordinary Giovannis and Giorgios. A current prominent surname bearer is Republican Congressman Tom Tancredo

Tane

TAH-NEH

Polynesian, mythology name

The name of the powerful Polynesian sky god who set the sun and moon in place and studded the heavens with stars: a majestic legacy for a simple yet unusual name.

Tanguy

tahn-gee

French, "warrior"

This engaging French saint's name, pronounced like tangy, with a hard 'g,' also has a creative connection to French surrealist painter Yves Tanguy.

Tarian

Welsh, "shield"

Country singer Travis Tritt is partial to the letter *T* for his children's names: he has a Tyler, a Tristan, and a son named Tarian. Tarian is a unisex Welsh name which, though used more for girls in Wales, would be perfectly acceptable here for a boy.

Tarquin

tar-kin

Roman clan name of uncertain meaning

One of the few ancient Roman names that doesn't end in *us*, the rarely heard Tarquin has a decidedly creative, even dramatic flair, which could appeal to the parent looking for a strikingly original name. Sir Laurence Olivier used it for his oldest child, who was named Simon Tarquin but called by his middle name.

As Tarquinius, it was borne by two early kings of Rome.

Tarquin has some literary cred as well, appearing in Shakespeare's poem *The Rape of Lucrece* (referring to a dark stain on the name), as Tarquin Blackwood in Anne Rice's *The Vampire Chronicles* series and as Tarquin Cleath-Stuart in the *Shopaholic* series by Sophie Kinsella.

Tavish

Scottish variation of Thomas, "twin"

This Scottish form of Thomas has a lot of charm, evoking images of men in plaid kilts playing the bagpipes. As for the 'ish' ending, it could either be seen as cozy and hamish, or a little wishy-washyish.

The Tavis version is associated these days with radio/TV personality Tavis Smiley.

Bottom line: If you're looking for a similar name with more ethnic appeal than Travis or an offbeat namesake for an ancestral Thomas, you could do well to consider Tavish.

Taye

African, Ethiopian, "he has been seen"

Taye, also used as a short form of Taylor, began to stand on its own with the emergence of actor Taye (born Scott) Diggs.

Tennessee

Native American, Cherokee, place-name

When playwright Thomas Lanier Williams adopted the pen name of Tennessee, he created a new possibility among American place-names, although it's admittedly a bit bulky in size. Rese Witherspoon brought it back into the spotlight when she chose it for her son.

Tertius

TER-shuss

Latin, "third"

Never as well known as that other Roman numeral name, Octavius, Tertius just might hold some appeal for the parent seeking a really obscure name with the patina of antiquity for her third son.

Tertius was an early Christian and a scribe whp assisted Paul in writing his epistle to the Romans. In George Eliot's *Middlemarch*, Tertius Lydgate is an idealistic doctor.

Thackeray

English, "place with thatching"

The name of the famous British man of letters might just appeal to some English majors as a more interesting alternative to Zachary. An appropriate playmate for Russell Crowe's boy Tennyson.

Thatcher

English occupational name, "roof thatcher"

Thatcher is an open and friendly freckle-faced surname, fresher sounding than Tyler or Taylor, that dates back to the days of thatched-roof cottages.

Britberries in particular may have strong associations to Prime Minister Margaret, but the surname has other notable bearers as well, such as Becky Thatcher, the object of Tom's affections in *The Adventures of Tom Sawyer*. Thatcher Grey is the protagonist's father on *Grey's Anatomy*, and TV celebrity chef Cat Cora has a son named Thatcher Julius.

Thayer

French variation of Taylor, "tailor"

Thayer is an affable, less-common alternative to Taylor, with a much more indirect connection to its occupational source. Actor Thayer David (born David

Thayer: Thayer was his father's first name) was known for his roles in *Rocky* and *Dark Shadows*.

Thelonious

Latinized variation of German Tillman, "one who plows the earth"

One of the coolest of names, thanks to legendary jazz pianist Thelonious Sphere Monk, who inherited this Latin-sounding German name from his father. It has been used very sparingly since the 1960's, with just a sprinkling of baby boys receiving the name each year.

Monk's middle name Sphere is pretty unique too — a cousin of Cosmos and Cosmo.

Theobald

German, "courageous people"

This is one of the least known or used of the Theo names, quite possibly because of its last syllable. In Samuel Butler's 1903 novel *The Way of All Flesh,"* there is a clergyman character named Theobald Pontifex.

You might want to consider the softer French version, Thibault (see below), or the Shakespearean Tybalt instead.

Theophilus

Greek, "loved by God" or "friend of God"

This is a multi-syllabic New Testament relic that could be yet another fresh way to get to Theo. In the beginning of Luke's gospel, he dedicates his words to Theophilus.

Theophilus North is the title of a novel by Thornton Wilder and the name of its protagonist.

Thibault

French from German, "courageous people"

Pronounced TEE-bow, this version, which is also a very common surname in France, has a lot more charm than the name it derives from — Theobald. A variant spelling is Thibaut.

Trivia tidbit: Thibault is the name of a minor character in *Peanuts*.

Thoreau

French literary name

This completely unique possibility evokes the calm and tranquility of Henry David Thoreau's Walden Pond.

Thorne

English, "thorn thicket"

Call your daughter Rose, but think twice about naming your son Thorne, which does have a bit of a soap opera feel — in fact there was a character named Thorne Forrester on *The Bold and the Beautiful* in the 1980's.

Thorne Smith (born James Thorne) was a comic fantasy writer most noted for his *Topper* novels.

Thurber

Norse, "Thor the warrior"

Pleasant surname connected to humorist James Thurber, with a sound as happy as a baby's gurgle.

Thurstan

Scandinavian, variation of Thurston, "Thor's stone"

Thurston Howell was the snooty millionaire on *Gilligan's Island*, but these days such surname names don't have the same elitist air.

Tiberius

Latin, "of the Tiber"

The name of an important ancient Roman emperor, Tiberius might sound a bit heavy for a modern boy to carry, but with the rise of Atticus, Tiberius and brothers begin to feel more baby-friendly, much in the same way as Old Testament names like Elijah and Isaiah have been rejuvenated.

The contemporary ear has become attuned to the name via some modern sagas. There were two Tiberiuses in the *Harry Potter* universe: T. McLaggen, uncle of Cormac, and T. Ogden, a former member of the Wizengamot. Peter O'Toole played Emperor Tiberius Caesar in the 1979 *Caligula*, and James Tiberius Kirk was Captain of the USS Enterprise on *Star Trek*.

Tibor

TEE-bore

Slavic, "sacred place"

Commonly heard in the Slavic countries, Tibor has a large measure of continental dash. On *The Simpsons*, Tibor is a non-English-speaking co-worker of Homer's at the Springfield Nuclear Power Plant.

Tiernan

Irish, "lord, chief"

Tiernan is the slightly edgier and more seductive cousin of Kiernan. This is one Irish surname that is attractive but distinctive; Tierney is another, related, option.

Tiernan was a popular name in early and medieval Ireland and was borne by several kings and saints. It is currently high on the list in Northern Ireland.

Tierney

Irish, "descendant of a lord"

Tierney is a Celtic surname with a definite Irish twinkle, a name just waiting to be discovered. Though now sometimes used for girls (in the US, not Ireland), as in jazz singer Tierney Sutton, it still has plenty of masculine punch.

Tierney, in its original Tiarnach form, was the name of several saints. It can also join the ranks of Old Hollywood names, via the haunting actress Gene Tierney. *ER* actress Maura Tierney is a current surname bearer.

Timeo

Italian from Greek, "honor"

Timeo is a Top 100 name in France but is virtually unknown in the English-speaking world. Appearing briefly in the New Testament and related to Timon, a Shakespearean name, Timeo is a valid possibility for parents looking for an unusual name with cross-cultural cred.

Tobiah

Hebrew, "the Lord is good"

Tobiah is the original Hebrew form of the better known Greek Tobias, to which it could make a distinctive alternative. With its *ah* ending, Tobiah fits in with other stylish Biblical names today, from Noah to Isaiah to Josiah and Zachariah. And of course, Toby is an adorable nickname.

Tolliver

English occupational name, "metalworker"

If you're tired of Oliver, you might consider this energetic three-syllable surname instead, so you could have a little Tolly instead of an Ollie.

Tolliver is a not-too-obvious occupational Scottish surname dating back to the time of armor makers. Heard much more often as a surname, there have been Tollivers in soap operas like *General Hospital* and Cy Tolliver was a character on *Deadwood*; in real life, Melba Tolliver is a barrier-breaking African-American TV journalist.

Torin

Irish, "chief"

Though it has a Scandinavian ring, this is an out-of-the-ordinary Irish family name. The hard '*T*' at the beginning prevents it from sounding as feminine as, say, Loren. *Torin's Passage* was an early video game.

Torquil

TOR-kil

Scottish from Norse, "Thor's cauldron"

Torquil, is a quirky but intriguing option that evolved from an ancient Scandinavian name and was imported into Scotland by the Vikings. The Gaelic form of the name is Torcaill.

Torquil MacLeod was the name of an early Scottish clan chief.

Tristram

Medieval English variation of Tristan, "riot, tumult"

This version of Tristan, known to English Lit students from the novel *Tristram Shandy*, is rarely used in this country, but, though its similarity to the popular Tristan could prove confusing, still makes an interesting literary choice.

Baseball legend Tris Speaker was christened Tristram and the protagonist of the Anthony Burgess novel *The Wanting Seed* is Tristram Foxe.

Truth

English word name

True has become an accepted first and middle name; Truth makes an even stronger statement.

Tully

Irish, "flood, peaceful, or hill"

Tully is a relaxed, rarely used Irish surname possibility. Sources disagree on the meaning, depending on what root is used. The Irish *tulach* means hill or mound, while *tuile* means flood. Other sources relate it to the Roman Tullius, most notably the name of the philosopher Marcus Tullius Cicero, sometimes anglicized as Tully. Statesman Alexander Hamilton used the pen name Tully when he wrote editorials denouncing the instigators of the Whiskey Rebellion.

The ancient Irish name Tuathal, which is translated as Tully, was given to many Irish kings and heroes.

Twain

English, "divided in two"

Twain can be thought of as a modernization (and possible namesake) of the dated Wayne, seasoned with the humor of Mark Twain, who adopted it from a river term.

U

Umberto

oom-BAIR-toe

Italian variation of Humbert, "renowned warrior"

A definite improvement over the English Humbert, Umberto has nevertheless been rarely heard outside the Italian community.

The writer-semiotician Umberto Eco is a noteworthy namesake.

Uziah

Hebrew, variant spelling of Uzziah, "Jehovah is my strength"

One of the most unusual of the biblical *iah*-options, this was the name of a long-reigning king of Judea, and just might appeal to the parent looking for a quasi-unique Old Testament choice. And it avoids the negative Dickensian aura of the other New Testament U-name, Uriah.

V

Valor

Word name

Honor and bravery are certainly virtues any parent would want to encourage, and this word itself is obscure enough that it manages to sound like a real name.

Vaughan

Welsh, "small"

This familiar but never popular Welsh surname name might be a good Sean alternative — and we're starting to hear some berrybuzz about it. Vaughn is an alternate spelling.

Three musical bearers of the name: British classical composer Ralph Vaughan Williams, 1940's US band leader and singer Vaughn Monroe and the great jazz vocalist Sarah Vaughan. And two more current surnamed Vaughans: comic actor Vince and musician Stevie Ray.

Verdi

Italian, "green"

This is an outside possibility for opera-lovers, with the additional eco/color factor.

Viggo

Scandinavian, "war"

Though to most Americans Viggo is a one-person name attached to intense actor Mortensen, it is actually an old Norse name dating back to the Vikings, and is currently the 32nd most popular appellation in Sweden. Viggo Mortensen is a Jr., sharing his name with his Danish father. We think this name is so, well, vigorous, that it might appeal to others as well. Taylor and Natalie Hanson seemed to agree when they chose it for their fourth child.

Vittorio

Italian variation of Victor, "conqueror"

Was there ever a name that rolled more appealingly off the tongue? Vittorio calls to mind the glory days of Italian cinema, featuring names like Vittorio de Sica and Vittorio Gassman.

Vladimir

Slavic, "renowned prince"

Vladimir, which has a musical prodigy kind of vibe, is a cultured Russian name associated in this country with piano virtuoso Vladimir Horowitz and the author of *Lolita*, Vladimir Nabokov.

Vladimir is rich in history as well, being the name of the first Christian ruler of Russia, who became the patron saint of that country's Catholic church; Lenin, the founder of the USSR, and current President Putin.

A common name throughout Russia, Vladimir is featured in novels by Turgenev and Pushkin. Vladimir also has vampirish connections: Dracula is based on Vlad III, otherwise known as — oops — Vlad the Impaler. A more modern literary character is Vladimir, one of the two main figures in Samuel Beckett's *Waiting for Godot*.

W

Wagner

German occupational name, "wagon maker"

Whether pronounced like the wag of a tail or as the correct German VAHG-ner, this might be something a devoted opera buff could consider as a middle name.

Wales

Place name

Place names for boys are few and far between; this one would make a singular choice. Prince William of Wales uses this as a surname when required, as in his military life; Jimmy Wales is the entrepreneur behind Wikipedia, Clint Eastwood played the eponymous character Josey (!) Wales in the 1976 *The Outlaw Josey Wales*.

Warrick

English, "fortress"

Warrick has recently come into the spotlight as a character on the TV show *CSI*. The more conventional spelling is Warwick, a medieval English noble name.

Westcott

English, "from the western cottage"

If you find West not substantial enough, this would make a more solid path to it.

Whittaker

English, "white field"

If you discount the connection to the controversial Whittaker Chambers in the days of the Red Scare, Whittaker is a pleasant enough British surname with the preppyish nickname Whit.

Wilder

Surname or word name

Though it hasn't yet appeared in the Top 1000, Wilder is on many parents' possibility lists, one of the new generation of bad boy names growing in popularity. Wilder got a big boost in interest through Goldie Hawn's grandson via son Oliver, born in 2007.

Wilder is more familiar as a surname, borne by such notables as authors Laura Ingalls and Thornton, composer Alex, director Billy, actor Gene, and Douglas Wilder, the first African-American to be elected Governor of Virginia.

Willem

Dutch variation of William, "resolute protector"

Common in Holland, the appealing Willem (as in de Kooning and Dafoe) makes William fresh and distinctive.

Willoughby

English, "farm near the willows"

Willoughby is an energetic last-name-first route to the popular short form Will, livelier than any of the two-syllable options. It could be picked up by parents attracted to the Willow sound for girls.

Willoughby Patterne is the protagonist of the George Meredith novel, *The Egotist*. Willoughby Sharp was a contemporary artist, curator, critic and founder of the seminal art magazine, *Avalanche*. There is a classic 1962 British children's novel titled *The Wolves of Willoughby Chase* by Joan Aiken that was made into a film in 1989.

Wim

v im

German, contracted form of Wilhelm, "resolute protector"

Film director Wim Wenders brought this to our attention; it certainly has vim and vigor.

Windsor

English, "riverbank with a winch"

Windsor has a variety of unisex references, including Britain's royal House of Windsor, Windsor Castle, a tie's windsor knot, as well as the Windsor Rose. In

1917, King George V adopted Windsor as the family surname, dropping the Germanic Saxe-Coburg and Gotha in the wake of World War I anti-German feeling.

Nicknames might include Win, Wind, Windy, and Winnie.

Winslow

English, "friend's hill or burial mound"

Winslow, despite its creative connection to the distinguished American painter Winslow Homer, does still retain remnants of the image of a Victorian boy in a sailor suit, making Winston or even just Win a preferable modern choice.

Winter

Word name

The girls have dibs on Spring, Summer, and Autumn, leaving this name evocative of snowy landscapes as the one possible seasonal choice for boys, even though it's been used for a couple of starbaby girls.

Wolf

German, "wolf"; diminutive of Wolfgang

Wolf is a name with a split personality. It can be seen as one of the fierce animal names, like Fox and Bear and Puma, with a touch of the werewolf, or it can be viewed as a quieter, Wolf Blitzer kind of name, fairly common in German (where is pronounced Vulf) and Jewish families, sometimes as a short form of Wolfgang.

CNN newscaster Blitzer inherited the name from his grandfather. Other Wolfs of note include British screenwriter Wolf Mankowitz, who was instrumental in the early James Bond films, painter Wolf Kahn, and the hero of Jack London's 1904 novel *The Sea-Wolf,* Wolf Larsen.

Nickname Wolfie definitely domesticates it.

Wyclef

English, "dweller at the white cliff"

Haitian-born rap superstar and humanitarian Wyclef ("Fugees") Jean has lent this name a powerful musical beat.

Wyn

Welsh, "fair, blessed"

Extremely popular in Wales, where it began as a nickname for someone who's fair, this name is winning even if it feels a bit close to the feminine Gwen and Winnie. Can also be spelled Wynn or Wynne.

X

Xerxes

Zerks-eeze

Persian, "hero among heroes"

The two X's may be a challenge for even the most intrepid baby namer. Xerxes was the name of two early kings of Persia and the Handel opera *Serse* or *Xerxes* is loosely based on Xerxes I.

Y

Yale

Welsh, "fertile upland"

An appellation that couldn't be more Ivy League — or sound less Welsh. The name of the University is taken from the surname of founder Elihu Yale. In the movie *Manhattan*, Yale Pollack is the name of Woody Allen's best friend. The Hebrew Yael is not related.

Yann

French/Breton variation of John, "God is gracious"

This might be a better choice than the similarly pronounced Jan, to avoid gender confusion.

Yeats

yates

English, "the gates"

Admirers of the haunting works of esteemed Irish poet and playwright William Butler Yeats might consider this, especially as a middle name.

Z

Zacharias

Greek form of Hebrew Zachariah, "the Lord has remembered"

One of several more venerable names that get to the nickname Zack if you're tired of Zachary. In the New Testament, Zacharias was the husband of Elizabeth and father of John the Baptist.

Zalman

Variation of Solomon, "peace"

More familiar now via its Salman form, thanks to author Rushdie; this is an unusual biblical alternative.

Zebedee

English variation of Hebrew Zebediah, "gift of God"

Zebedee is an adorable and unusual New Testament name — which may sound like but is not a contradiction in terms. Unlike some of the longer biblical Z-names, Zebedee has a more lighthearted usability, with its gleeful *ee*-ending. And Zeb makes a fabulous nickname.

In the New Testament, Zebediah/Zebedeee plays the major role of the fisherman father of two disciples, James and John, and was with his sons mending his fishing nets when they were called by Christ.

The name was popularized in the UK by a jack-in-the-box puppet named Zebedee on an early kids' TV show, *The Magic Roundabout*.

Zebedee Jones is a contemporary British painter.

Zebediah

Hebrew, "gift of Jehovah"

Biblical names are expanding (literally) as some parents move from Isaiah and Elijah to more elaborate choices with simple short forms, like Jedidiah and Zebediah.

Zebediah, or Zebadiah, is the New Testament father of apostles John and James, and there are a number of Zebadiahs in the Old Testament as well.

Zedekiah

zeh-deh-KY-uh

Hebrew, "the Lord is just"

The name of an Old Testament king, and yet another 'Z' choice from the Bible that still retains some zip, especially with the appealing nickname Zed. Zedekiah was the name of the last king of Judea before the city was destroyed by Babylon.

Zelig

Yiddish variation of Selig, "blessed, happy"

A plausible choice — if it can ever shake off its ubiquitous-guy Woody Allen identity.

Zen

Japanese, form of Buddhism

A spiritual word name used by actor Corey Feldman for his son.

Zeo

Modern invented name

More neo than Neo, this is a name heard in the Power Rangers film title *Power Rangers Zeo*.

Zephyr

Greek, "west wind"

If you're looking for a boy's name that's light and breezy, this could be it. A name from mythology: Zephyrus/Zephyr was the Greek god of the west wind — with many European variations, it's a name that's frequently seen in computer and video games, is a character in the children's book *Silverwing*, and appears in the *Babar* books — as a monkey.

Robby Benson and Karla De Vito named their son Zephyr in 1992, and Zephyr Benson is now a fledgling actor himself.

Zephyrin

French variation of Zephyr, "west wind"

This name feels warmer and more human-appropriate in its longer version, but still retains that breezy feel. Trivia tidbit: Zephyrinus was a Jewish pope.

Zeus

Greek mythology name

The supreme Olympian god represents a mighty image for a little fella to live up to, but more and more parents are beginning to consider it seriously. The Roman equivalent Jupiter has also come down to earth.

Zubin

Persian, "short spear"

This is most familiar here as a musical name, via Indian Parsi conductor Zubin Mehta, but it certainly could be used by others.

THE COMPLETE LIST

GIRLS

Aada	Adamina	Agyness	Alaia
Aalia	Adara	Ahava	Alair
Aanisah	Adasha	Aibhilin	Alala
Abalina	Addah	Aidan	Alameda
Abbetina	Adecyn	Aideen	Alanis
Abbott	Adelei	Aiden	Albany
Abelia	Adelpha	Aiko	Albia
Abena	Adelphia	Ailani	Albinia
Aberdeen	Adema	Ailbhe	Alchamy
Abia	Adhara	Ailis	Alchemy
Abiela	Adine	Ailsa	Alcott
Abijah	Adira	Aimée	Alcyone
Abilene	Adolpha	Aimilios	Alden
Abital	Adora	Aine	Aleela
Abitha	Aeliana	Áine	Aleeza
Abra	Aenea	Ainhoa	Alek
Abrial	Aerin	Air	Alessia
Abriana	Aeron	Aishwarya	Alexandrina
Abt	Affinity	Aisling	Alexane
Abyssinia	Afia	Aislinn	Alexx
Acacia	Afra	Aitana	Alfonsine
Acadia	Africa	Aithne	Alhambra
Acantha	Afternoon	Akako	Aliena
Accalia	Agapi	Akasha	Alienor
Adair	Agate	Akilah	Alika
Adalia	Agrippina	Akiva	Alix

Alizabeth	Amerie	Annamaria	Aquitaine
Alizée	Amethyst	Anne-Marie	Arabesque
Alizeh	Amica	Annia	Arabia
Allaire	Amidala	Annik	Arantxa
Allegra	Aminta	Anniston	Arava
Allegro	Amita	Annistyn	Aravis
Allura	Amity	Annora	Arbor
Almond	Amoret	Annunciata	Arcadia
Alohi	Amoris	Anouck	Arcangela
Aloisa	Amory	Anouk	Arcelia
Aloisia	Anaelle	Anoush	Archer
Alouette	Anahí	Anoushka	Arda
Alto	Anahita	Ansel	Arddun
Alton	Anaïs	Ansonia	Arella
Alula	Anala	Answer	Argenta
Alura	Analisa	Anthea	Argentia
Alya	Anamaria	Antigone	Argentina
Alyanna	Ananda	Antiquity	Ari
Alyenor	Anatola	Antonella	Ariadne
Alyona	Andi	Ántonia	Arianne
Alzbet	Andorra	Anwen	Arianwen
Alzea	Andrée	Anzu	Arianwyn
Amabel	Andromeda	Aobh	Arissa
Amadea	Aneko	Aoi	Arista
Amadi	Anemone	Aoibh	Ariza
Amaia	Angélique	Aoibhe	Arleigh
Amalfi	Angelou	Aoibheann	Arlenis
Amalya	Angharad	Aoibhinn	Arlette
Amandine	Ani	Aoife	Arlise
Amarantha	Aniceta	Aphra	Arlo
Amariah	Anina	Aphrodite	Armande
Amarissa	Anisa	Apollonia	Armantine
Amaryllis	Anise	Apple	Armel
Amata	Anisha	Aqua	Armina
Ambrosia	Anja	Aquarius	Arnelle
Amedea	Anju	Aquilia	Arno
Amélie	Annalie	Aquilina	Aroa
Amena	Annalisa	Aquinnah	Arpina

Arria	Aurex	Bala	Bedelia
Arsenia	Auria	Baldwin	Beeja
Artemis	Auriel	Bali	Begonia
Arthur	Aurinda	Ballencia	Behati
Artis	Austen	Ballou	Beibhinn
Arusha	Austria	Bambalina	Beige
Arverne	Avalon	Banana	Bela
Arwen	Avani	Bao	Belén
Arza	Aveline	Baptista	Beline
Asa	Averil	Bara	Bellatrix
Asante	Averill	Baraka	Bellerose
Ascella	Avita	Barbro	Bellezza
Asencion	Aviva	Barcelona	Beloved
Ash	Avril	Bardot	Benedetta
Ashby	Axelle	Bariah	Benedicta
Ashira	Ayelet	Barrett	Benicia
Asma	Ayn	Barrie	Benilde
Assisi	Ayu	Barry	Benjamina
Asta	Aza	Basha	Bennington
Aster	Azalea	Basilia	Berit
Astera	Azami	Bathsheba	Bermuda
Astoria	Azar	Bathshira	Bernarda
Astra	Azenor	Batya	Berry
Atalanta	Azha	Bay	Bertille
Atara	Aziza	Baya	Bertrice
Atarah	Azni	Bayleah	Beta
Athalia	Azuba	Bayley	Bethan
Atherton	Azure	Baylor	Bethesda
Atia	Babe	Bayo	Bethia
Atlanta	Baez	Bayou	Bethoc
Atlantis	Bahaar	Beah	Betta
Atria	Bahia	Beata	Bevin
Auberon	Bahira	Beatha	Beyoncé
Auburn	Bai	Beathag	Bibi
Aud	Baia	Becca	Bibiana
Auden	Baila	Bechet	Bice
August	Baize	Bechette	Bichette
Aurelius	Baja	Beck	Biddy

Bidelia	Brid	Cai	Cappella
Bidu	Bride	Caia	Capri
Bienvenida	Brie	Cailin	Capucine
Bijou	Brienna	Caily	Carbry
Binnie	Brighid	Cairo	Carden
Bionda	Brighton	Cait	Caridad
Birgit	Brigidine	Caitriona	Carita
Björk	Brilie	Cala	Carlin
Blaine	Brinsley	Calais	Carlisle
Blakesleigh	Brio	Calandra	Caroun
Blaque	Briona	Calantha	Carter
Blaze	Briony	Calder	Carys
Bleu	Britannia	Caledonia	Cascade
Bliss	Brónach	Calico	Cashmere
Blodwen	Bronnen	Calida	Caspian
Blue	Bronte	California	Cass
Bluebell	Brontë	Calixta	Cassia
Bluma	Bronwen	Callas	Cassiopeia
Blythe	Bronwyn	Calliope	Cat
Boheme	Bronya	Callista	Cate
Bohemia	Bruna	Calvina	Caterina
Bolivia	Brunhild	Calypso	Cathay
Bonanza	Brunhilda	Cam	Catriona
Bora	Bryce	Cambrie	Cayenne
Boudicca	Brycin	Camden	Ceara
Bradley	Brylie	Camellia	Cedar
Brady	Brynna	Cameo	Cela
Brae	Bryony	Camera	Celinda
Braeden	Bunny	Campana	Cella
Branwen	Buona	Canada	Cerelia
Brasilia	Burgundy	Canary	Ceres
Brayden	Burma	Candela	Ceridwen
Brazil	Buttercup	Cantara	Cerise
Breeze	Butterfly	Cantata	Cerulean
Brennan	Cachet	Cantrelle	Cerulia
Briallen	Cadeau	Canyon	Cerys
Briar	Cadenza	Caoimhe	Cesaria
Brice	Cady	Capella	Cessair

Ceylon	Ciel	Colombine	Curry
Cézanne	Cimarron	Colorado	Curtis
Chabelly	Cimmaron	Columba	Cyan
Chabely	Cinderella	Comet	Cyane
Chablis	Cinnabar	Comfort	Cybele
Chakra	Cipriana	Como	Cyder
Chambray	Circe	Concepciòn	Cylia
Chamois	Citron	Conchita	Cynara
Chan	Clancy	Concordia	Cypress
Chanah	Clarence	Condoleezza	Cyra
Chandelle	Claret	Connelly	Cyril
Channel	Clarion	Connemara	Cyrilla
Chanson	Clarity	Connolly	Cyrille
Chantilly	Clea	Connor	Cytherea
Chara	Clelia	Conor	Dacey
Chardonnay	Clematis	Constantina	Dacia
Charis	Clemencia	Constanza	Dael
Charisma	Clemency	Copper	Daffodil
Charmian	Clemensia	Corazòn	Dagan
Charna	Cleopatra	Corbin	Dahliana
Charo	Clia	Cordis	Dai
Charra	Cliantha	Corin	Daisi
Charty	Clio	Corisande	Dakira
Chauncey	Cliona	Coro	Dalila
Chava	Clodagh	Corona	Dalili
Chela	Clor	Corsica	Damara
Chesleigh	Clorinda	Corvina	Damia
Chesney	Clothilde	Cosette	Damiana
Chiara	Cloud	Cosima	Damiane
Chihiro	Clove	Countess	Damica
Chiqueta	Clover	Crescent	Damita
Chiyo	Cobalt	Cressida	Danaë
Chloris	Coco	Cricket	Dancer
Christabel	Cocoa	Crimson	Dane
Christia	Coe	Crisanta	Danique
Christmas	Colby	Crispina	Danit
Christo	Coline	Cruise	Danu
Cia	Colombia	Curran	Danube

Dany	Demeter	Diversity	Duffy
Danya	Democracy	Divina	Dulcia
Dari	Deni	Divine	Dune
Dariel	Denver	Divinity	Dunya
Dariela	Dervla	Dodie	Dusana
Darrell	Deryn	Doe	Duscha
Darren	Desdemona	Domini	Dusha
Darsha	Desi	Dominica	Dustin
Daru	Desirée	Dominik	Dwyn
Darva	Destry	Domino	Dwynwen
Darya	Deva	Domitilla	Dyani
Dash	Devi	Domitille	Dylana
Dasha	Devora	Donata	Eabha
Dashawna	Devorah	Donatella	Eachna
Datyah	Dex	Donnelly	Eagle
Davida	Dexter	Doon	Earhart
Day	Dhana	Doré	Earla
Daya	Dhara	Doria	Early
Dayaa	Dharma	Dorian	East
Dayo	Dia	Dorit	Easton
Dayton	Diablo	Dorkas	Eavan
Dearbhail	Diahann	Doro	Eban
Debs	Diamanta	Dorsey	Ebele
December	Diantha	Dory	Eccentricity
Decima	Diarra	Douce	Ecru
Decla	Diaz	Douglas	Edana
Déja	Didi	Doutzen	Edda
Delancey	Dido	Doveva	Edina
Délice	Digna	Drea	Edlyn
Delicia	Dija	Dream	Edwige
Delight	Dillian	Dree	Eglantine
Delise	Dillon	Dru	Egle
Delja	Dilly	Druella	Egypt
Dellen	Dilys	Drum	Eibhlin
Delphi	Dimanche	Duana	Eila
Deltha	Dior	Duane	Eilidh
Delyth	Discovery	Dudee	Eilis
Demelza	Diva	Duff	Eilish

Eimear	Ellery	Enora	Fabienne
Eir	Ellington	Enrica	Fable
Eira	Elliott	Enterprise	Fabrizia
Éire	Ellison	Enya	Faine
Eirian	Elm	Eowyn	Fairfax
Eithne	Eloquent	Épiphanie	Fairuza
Ekat	Elsbeth	Erga	Faizah
Ekaterina	Elske	Ernest	Falala
Elara	Elspeth	Eroica	Falcon
Electra	Elula	Errol	Faline
Elektra	Eluned	Eshe	Famke
Eleni	Elya	Etana	Fana
Eleonara	Elysia	Étaoin	Fanchon
Eleri	Emani	Eternity	Fancy
Elethea	Embeth	Ethereal	Fania
Elettra	Embry	Ethical	Fannia
Eleven	Emeny	Ethne	Fantasia
Elexis	Emer	Étoile	Fantine
Elfrida	Émer	Etude	Fanya
Elga	Emese	Eurydice	Farasha
Eliane	Emiliana	Eustacia	Farida
Éliane	Emina	Evadne	Farrell
Elias	Emira	Evan	Fauna
Elidi	Emlyn	Evanna	Faunia
Elif	Emmalynn	Evanthe	Fausta
Elili	Emmanuelle	Evella	Faustina
Eliora	Emme	Evening	Faustine
Eliot	Emmeline	Everest	Favor
Elisabet	Emmet	Everett	Fayola
Elisabetta	Emmett	Every	Feather
Elisheva	Emmi	Evian	Federica
Eliska	Emmylou	Evrose	Fedora
Elixyvett	Endeavor	Experience	Fee
Elixyvette	Energy	Explorer	Felicidad
Elizabella	England	Ezra	Felixa
Elizabetta	Engracia	Ezri	Fenella
Elka	Enjoli	Fabia	Fennel
Elke	Ennis	Fabiana	Feodora

Ferebee	Ford	Galla	Ginevra
Fergie	Forever	Galway	Gioconda
Fernande	Forsythia	Galya	Gioia
Fey	Fortunata	Ganesha	Giordana
Ffion	Fortune	Gannet	Gish
Fflur	Foxy	Ganya	Gita
Fia	Franca	Garbo	Gitana
Fiammetta	France	Garcelle	Giuditta
Fianna	Françoise	Garcia	Giulia
Fideline	Frankie-Jean	Gardener	Giuseppina
Fidelity	Franny	Gardenia	Glade
Fife	Frayda	Gardner	Glasgow
Fifer	Frederique	Garin	Glenys
Fifi	Free	Garland	Glimmer
Fig	Freedom	Gauri	Glory
Filipa	Freesia	Gavi	Goddess
Finch	Freja	Gayelette	God'iss
Finella	Freya	Gaynor	Godiva
Finlay	Fritzi	Gazella	Goya
Finn	Fritzie	Geela	Grady
Finola	Frost	Geena	Grainne
Finula	Frostine	Gelsey	Gráinne
Fionnuala	Fuchsia	Gemini	Granada
Fiorella	Fulvia	Gen	Grande
Firth	Future	Geneen	Grania
Fjord	Fyodora	Generosity	Gravity
Flair	Gabi	Gennifer	Gray
Flame	Gaenor	Genoa	Grazia
Flanna	Gaetana	Gentry	Graziana
Flannery	Gaia	Georgeanne	Graziella
Flavie	Gala	Geranium	Green
Fleur	Galatea	Gerardine	Greer
Florentina	Galaxy	Gervaise	Greige
Flory	Galen	Ghislaine	Grier
Flower	Gali	Giacinta	Grove
Floyd	Galila	Gila	Gucci
Flynn	Galilee	Gilberte	Gudrun
Folami	Galina	Gin	Guernsey

Guevara	Harika	Honey	Ilsa
Guinevere	Harlem	Honor	Ilse
Guitar	Harmonia	Honoria	Iluminada
Gull	Hartley	Honorine	Imagine
Gundruna	Harum	Horatia	Imajica
Gunhilda	Hatsy	Hoshi	Imala
Gunilla	Hava	Howard	Iman
Gus	Havana	Huali	Imara
Gustava	Havilah	Hudson	Imena
Guthrie	Haviva	Huyana	Immaculada
Gwendolen	Haya	Hyacinth	Immy
Gwenore	Haydée	Hye	Imogen
Gwyneira	Hea	Hypatia	Imperia
Gwynn	Heavenly	Ian	Inaya
Gypsy	Hebe	Ianthe	Inbar
Habibah	Hecuba	Ibby	Indah
Hadar	Hedda	Iberia	Indigo
Hadiya	Helia	Idalah	Indira
Hagar	Helisent	Idalina	Indra
Haidee	Heloise	Idina	Indre
Hala	Héloïse	Idony	Indu
Halcyon	Helsa	Idra	Inessa
Haldis	Henna	Ieesha	Infinity
Halia	Hephzibah	Iekeliene	Inoa
Halimah	Hepzibah	Ife	Inocencia
Halona	Hera	Ignacia	Inspiration
Halsey	Hermia	Iida	Integrity
Hanako	Hermione	Ikea	Io
Hani	Hermosa	Ilana	Ioanna
Hania	Hero	Ilaria	Iolana
Hanifa	Hialeah	Ilena	Iolani
Hanita	Hilaria	Ilesha	Iolanthe
Hannelore	Himalaya	Ilisa	Ionia
Happy	Hiroko	Ilise	Ioulia
Haqikah	Hjördis	Ilisha	Iphigenia
Hara	Holiday	Ilka	Irati
Harbor	Holland	Illumination	Irie
Hariata	Honesty	Illuminée	Irina

Isabeau	Jadine	Jenica	Jonquil
Isabetta	Jadon	Jenifry	Jora
Isak	Jael	Jennet	Jordana
Isaline	Jaffa	Jennison	Jorie
Isannah	Jakarta	Jensine	Josepha
Isaura	Jala	Jentry	Joss
Iselin	Jalajaa	Jeremine	Josselyn
Isha	Jalen	Jericho	Jovana
Ishana	Jalila	Jersey	Jovie
Ishi	Jamaica	Jess	Juba
Islay	Jamesina	Jessamine	Jubilee
Isle	Jameson	Jessamy	Jude
Ismay	Jamilla	Jessamyn	Jules
Ismene	Jamison	Jet	Julienne
Isolde	Janan	Jethra	Julietta
Ita	Janeane	Jette	Julitta
Italia	Janica	Jeune	Julitte
Ithaca	Janka	Jezebel	July
Iúile	Janne	Jin	Jumana
Iulia	Janvier	Jinan	Juna
Iuliana	Jarah	Jinja	Juneau
Iulija	Jarita	Jinx	Juni
Ivanka	Jarrell	Jivanta	Juno
Ivara	Jaunel	Joaquina	Kacia
Ivria	Java	Jobeth	Kadida
Iyabo	Javiera	Jobina	Kady
Izara	Jay	Joby	Kaena
Izaro	Jaya	Jocasta	Kahlo
Izusa	Jaz	Joëlle	Kalama
Izzy	Jazz	Joely	Kalila
Jacaranda	Jelena	Johnnie	Kalinda
Jacelyn	Jelina	Joie	Kalindi
Jacinda	Jellia	Jojo	Kallan
Jacinta	Jelsa	Jola	Kalliope
Jacoba	Jem	Jolán	Kallista
Jacobina	Jemini	Jolanda	Kama
Jacquetta	Jemsa	Jolanta	Kamala
Jacy	Jenessa	Jonet	Kamali

Kamaria	Keziah	Lakshmi	Lex
Kanika	Khadija	Lalage	Lexia
Kanya	Khalida	Lalia	Lexy
Karena	Kiaria	Lalita	Leya
Karlyn	Kieran	Lally	Lian
Kasen	Kiki	Lamia	Lianne
Kashmir	Kimana	Lane	Libertad
Kasia	Kimba	Langley	Libra
Kat	Kimi	Lapis	Lidda
Katell	Kinga	Laragh	Lido
Katniss	Kiona	Laras	Liesa
Kato	Kiranda	Larisa	Liesl
Katti	Kiri	Lark	Ligeia
Katya	Kiriah	Larkin	Lil
Keagan	Kirsi	Lauralei	Lilac
Keaton	Kismet	Laurence	Lileas
Keats	Kissa	Laurentia	Liliane
Keegan	Kit	Laurenza	Lilias
Keela	Kitron	Lavanda	Lilibeth
Keelin	Kiva	Lavender	Lillias
Keenan	Klee	Lawrence	Lilo
Keiko	Kodiak	Leaf	Lilou
Keil	Kody	Leela	Linden
Keilah	Koffi	Leelee	Linnéa
Keith	Koko	Leeza	Linnet
Kelda	Kosma	Legend	Linnett
Kelila	Krishna	Leire	Lionel
Kelilah	Kristiana	Leith	Livana
Kerani	Krizia	Leni	Liya
Keren	Kyoko	Leocadia	Lizanne
Kerensa	Kyoto	Léonie	Llio
Kerr	Laelia	Leontyne	Lloyd
Kerris	Laetitia	Les	Locklyn
Kessie	Laguna	Lester	Loire
Keturah	Laia	Letesha	Lolo
Kevyn	Lainie	Letizia	Lorca
Kew	Lake	Lettice	Lorelle
Kezia	Lakota	Levia	Lotus

Louisianna	Madrigal	Malin	Mariota
Lowri	Madrona	Malina	Mariposa
Luanda	Maelie	Malka	Maris
Luba	Maelle	Mallorca	Mariska
Luca	Maelys	Malou	Marit
Lucasta	Maeva	Malta	Mariya
Lucerne	Magaidh	Malu	Marjani
Lucida	Magda	Malva	Marlin
Lucienne	Magee	Mandara	Marlon
Lucilla	Magenta	Mandolin	Marlow
Lucine	Magic	Mandoline	Marlowe
Lucky	Mago	Manet	Marsh
Ludmila	Magritte	Manette	Marshall
Ludovica	Mahogany	Manon	Martia
Luise	Maikki	Manzie	Martin
Luiza	Maile	Maple	Marvin
Lumière	Maillol	Marabel	Marya
Lurleen	Mailys	Maraca	Masha
Lux	Maine	Marah	Mason
Lydda	Maire	Marbella	Massima
Lyle	Mairead	Marcellina	Matalin
Lynwen	Mairéad	March	Matisse
Lyra	Mairi	Marcheline	Mattea
Lysistrata	Maisie	Marciana	Maurelle
Lystra	Maize	Mardi	Maury
Maaza	Maja	Mare	Maurya
Mab	Majesty	Mareike	Mauve
Mabs	Majken	Margalo	Max
Mabyn	Majorca	Margaux	Maxi
Macaria	Makani	Margit	Maxima
Macen	Makara	Margolette	Mayim
Macha	Makeda	Mariella	Mead
Machiko	Makelesi	Marielle	Meara
Macon	Makena'lei	Marigold	Medea
Maddie	Malagueña	Marika	Medrie
Madeira	Malgosia	Marimba	Meena
Madelaine	Mali	Marine	Megumi
Madigan	Malika	Marini	Mehira

Mehitabel	Mica	Mo	Naava
Mehri	Micheline	Moa	Nabila
Mei	Michiko	Mocha	Nadalia
Meike	Micki	Modesty	Nadida
Meissa	Midge	Monday	Nadira
Mel	Midori	Monet	Nadya
Mela	Mieko	Moon	Nagida
Melanctha	Miguela	Mór	Nahara
Melania	Mika	Morag	Naia
Melantha	Mikhaila	Mórag	Naiara
Melia	Miki	Morgana	Naida
Meliora	Mikki	Morley	Nairi
Melisande	Mikko	Morna	Nairne
Mélisande	Milada	Morning	Nairobi
Melisende	Milla	Moroccan	Naja
Melisent	Millay	Morocco	Najah
Melita	Milton	Morris	Najiba
Melora	Mim	Morrisania	Najila
Memphis	Mimosa	Morven	Nakotah
Merce	Min	Morwenna	Nala
Mercer	Mindel	Moselle	Nalani
Mercury	Minette	Mosley	Nanon
Merel	Minuet	Moxie	Nantale
Meri	Mio	Mucia	Naoko
Meriall	Mirabel	Muguet	Nara
Meribah	Mirabella	Muirgen	Narcissa
Meriel	Mirabelle	Munro	Narda
Merilee	Mireia	Murphy	Naretha
Merona	Mireille	Murran	Narnia
Merrigan	Mirin	Murray	Naroa
Merrill	Miró	Muse	Narva
Merritt	Mirra	Musetta	Nascha
Merryn	Mirren	Music	Nashawna
Mesa	Mirtha	Myfanwy	Nashira
Messiah	Mischa	Mystery	Nashota
Mette	Misha	Mystique	Nasia
Miami	Mitra	Naamah	Nasima
Miata	Miuccia	Naarah	Nastassia

Natalija	Nephele	Nilla	Oak
Natania	Neptune	Nima	Oakley
Natashya	Nera	Ninetta	Oba
Natividad	Nere	Ninon	Obedience
Nava	Nerea	Niobe	Obelia
Navi	Neriah	Nirvana	Oberon
Navy	Nerida	Nisha	O'brien
Nayana	Nerilla	Nissa	Oceana
Nayara	Nerine	Niva	Oceane
Nayo	Nerissa	Nixi	Océane
Nazaret	Nerys	Nixie	October
Nazelli	Nessa	Nizana	Odeda
Nazira	Nesta	Noa	Odele
Nazy	Nevara	Noah	Odetta
Neal	Neve	Noelani	Ofira
Neala	Neves	Noely	Ofra
Nebula	Neviah	Noemí	Ohanna
Nechama	Nevis	Noémie	Ohara
Nedda	Newlyn	Nolita	O'keeffe
Neeja	Ngaio	Nolwenn	Oksana
Neel	Ngozi	Nonn	Olea
Neela	Niabi	Noor	Olesia
Neele	Niamh	Norabel	Oliana
Neema	Niani	Nordica	Oluchi
Neesha	Niara	Nori	Olwen
Nefertiti	Nica	Norris	Olwyn
Nehama	Nicasia	North	Olya
Neil	Nico	Nouvel	Omaira
Neila	Nicolina	November	Omarosa
Neima	Nidia	Nuala	Omega
Neith	Nieves	Nunzia	Ondine
Nekane	Nigella	Nuria	Ondrea
Nellary	Nik	Nuru	Oneonta
Nemea	Nika	Nyala	Ono
Nemy	Nike	Nydia	Onóra
Nenna	Nikeesha	Nyomi	Onyx
Neo	Nile	Nyssa	Oona
Neorah	Niley	Nyx	Opera

Ophelie	Owen	Pascale	Pernella
Ophélie	Ozara	Pascoe	Perouze
Ophira	Ozma	Pascua	Perpetua
Oprah	Paccia	Pasha	Perrine
Orabella	Pace	Patia	Persephone
Oracia	Pacey	Patrizia	Persia
Oralie	Paciencia	Patzi	Persis
Orane	Pacifica	Paule	Peru
Orange	Padget	Paulille	Pessa
Orchid	Padma	Pavana	Peta
Orella	Page	Pavati	Petah
Oriana	Paili	Pavla	Petal
Oriel	Pakuna	Pax	Petula
Orina	Palantina	Paxton	Petulia
Orinda	Palasha	Payson	Petunia
Orino	Palila	Paz	Phaedra
Orinthia	Palin	Paziah	Phedora
Oriole	Pallas	Peace	Phila
Orion	Palmira	Peaches	Philadelphia
Orit	Palomina	Pecola	Philippa
Orla	Pamina	Pedra	Philippine
Orlanda	Panama	Peg	Phillida
Orleanna	Pandara	Pegeen	Philomela
Orli	Pandita	Pelagia	Phyllida
Ormanda	Pania	Pele	Phynley
Orna	Panna	Pella	Pia
Ororo	Panthea	Penina	Piaf
Orpah	Panya	Penna	Piala
Orphea	Paolina	Penrose	Picabia
Orsa	Papatya	Pensée	Picabo
Ortensia	Paquita	Penthia	Pierette
Osaka	Paradice	Peony	Pilar
Osanna	Parasha	Pepita	Pili
Ottaline	Parastoo	Percy	Pippa
Ottavia	Pari	Perdita	Pippi
Otthild	Parisa	Perfecta	Pixie
Ottoline	Parmenia	Peri	Placida
Ouisa	Parvati	Peridot	Plácida

Placidia	Qadira	Rainey	Reign
Pleasant	Qiturah	Rainie	Reignbeau
Plum	Quadeisha	Raisa	Reignbow
Po	Quanda	Raizel	Reiko
Poe	Quarry	Raja	Réka
Poesy	Quartilla	Rajani	Remarkable
Poet	Quenby	Rakel	Remember
Poetry	Querida	Raleigh	Remi
Polexia	Questa	Rama	Remington
Polina	Quilla	Ramana	Ren
Pollyanna	Quince	Ramira	Renate
Pomme	Quincy	Rana	Renée
Pomona	Quintana	Randa	Renesmee
Poppy	Quintessa	Randolph	Renny
Porter	Quintessence	Rani	Reseda
Posey	Quintia	Ranielle	Reuelle
Posy	Quintina	Ranita	Revel
Prairie	Quirina	Raniyah	Reverie
Praise	Raanana	Raphaela	Rexanne
Praxis	Rabanne	Rashanda	Reynold
Preciosa	Rabia	Ratih	Rez
Prima	Rabiah	Ravenna	Rhapsody
Primavera	Rada	Raya	Rheya
Primrose	Radella	Raylan	Rhian
Primula	Radeyah	Raymonda	Rhonwen
Priya	Radhiya	Raysel	Rhya
Promise	Radiah	Raz	Ria
Provence	Radinka	Raziah	Rialta
Pru	Radmila	Raziela	Riana
Prune	Raee	Razili	Riane
Prunella	Rafa	Raziya	Rica
Psyche	Raffaela	Rea	Richarda
Pua	Raga	Rebekka	Rikku
Puck	Rai	Red	Rilian
Puebla	Raidah	Reed	Rima
Puma	Rain	Reeve	Rimona
Purity	Rainbow	Reggie	Rin
Putri	Raine	Reginy	Rio

Riona	Rudy	Sameh	Sebastiane
Ripley	Rue	Sameria	Secret
Rishi	Rufina	Sami	Sedona
Rishona	Rumer	Samoa	Seeley
Riva	Ruri	Samuela	Sefarina
Rivage	Russet	Sana	Sela
Roanna	Russia	Sanchia	Selby
Robbia	Rut	Sancia	Selima
Robina	Rylea	Sandrine	Sen
Roderica	Ryo	Sania	Senalda
Rohan	Sabah	Sanna	Seneca
Rohana	Sacha	Sanne	Senegal
Roisin	Sadhbh	Saoirse	Senga
Róisín	Sadira	Sapphira	Senna
Roksana	Sadiya	Sapphire	Senta
Romana	Saffron	Sappho	Sephora
Romane	Safiyya	Saralee	September
Romilly	Saga	Sardinia	Septima
Romina	Sahar	Sari	Sequoia
Romney	Sahara	Sascha	Sequoyah
Romola	Sahteene	Saskia	Sera
Romy	Sai	Sassandra	Serafima
Ronalda	Sailor	Satchel	Serafina
Ronia	Saison	Satin	Seraphina
Ronja	Sakura	Satine	Seraphine
Ronni	Sala	Satyana	Seren
Rosae	Salama	Savita	Serenade
Rosalba	Salana	Saylah	Serendipity
Rosaleen	Salem	Scarla	Sergia
Rosamund	Salima	Schuyler	Serleena
Roscoe	Salmon	Scirocco	Serra
Roselle	Salvadora	Scotia	Sesame
Rosellen	Salvia	Scotland	Seth
Rosemond	Sam	Scotty	Sethe
Roux	Samala	Scout	Seven
Royce	Samanda	Scyler	Severina
Roza	Samar	Seana	Severine
Rubì	Samaria	Season	Sevilla

Seymour	Sidonia	Solange	Sulola
Shada	Sidonie	Soleil	Sumi
Shadow	Sidony	Solene	Sun
Shafira	Sidra	Solita	Suri
Shakila	Signy	Solveig	Suria
Shakti	Sigourney	Sonata	Surya
Shalom	Silas	Sonatina	Suvi
Shalona	Síle	Sonnet	Svetlana
Shalyn	Silence	Sonoma	Swanhild
Shamara	Silke	Sonora	Sweden
Shamira	Silken	Sookie	Sweeney
Shantal	Silver	Soraya	Sylvana
Shanti	Simonetta	Sorcha	Sylvie
Shany	Simplicity	Sorrel	Symphony
Shaquilla	Sincere	Sorrell	Sy'rai
Sharai	Sincerity	Sosie	Tabia
Sharpay	Sinclair	Sparrow	Taci
Shaula	Síne	Spencer	Tacita
Shaw	Sinead	Spirit	Tacy
Shayne	Sinéad	Spruce	Tadita
Sheba	Siobahn	Stam	Taffeta
Sheherazade	Siobhán	Stanley	Taffy
Sheldon	Siran	Starling	Tahira
Shell	Sirena	Steel	Tahiti
Shevonne	Siri	Steena	Tahnee
Shia	Siria	Stefanya	Tahoe
Shifra	Sisley	Sterling	Taj
Shirin	Sissy	Stina	Takala
Shivani	Sistine	Stockard	Takara
Shoshana	Sixtine	Storm	Tala
Shoushan	Slate	Story	Tali
Shula	Snejana	Strawberry	Taliesin
Shulamit	Snow	Stuart	Talila
Shura	Snow	Subira	Taline
Sian	Socorra	Sugar	Talisa
Sibley	Sofi	Sukey	Talitha
Sicily	Sojourner	Suki	Tallie
Sidda	Solana	Sullivan	Tallulah

Tally	Tazu	Tiernan	Tuesday
Talma	Téa	Tierney	Tulip
Talula	Teal	Tijuana	Tullia
Talulla	Tegwen	Tikvah	Tulsa
Talullah	Tehila	Tilly	Tundra
Talya	Telma	Timea	Turia
Tamah	Tempest	Timothea	Turquoise
Tamako	Temple	Tindra	Tuva
Tamar	Tempo	Tinsley	Tyas
Tamarind	Tenzin	Tipper	Tycen
Tamayo	Teodora	Tira	Tyne
Tamora	Tequila	Tirzah	Tyson
Tamsin	Terencia	Tish	Tzipora
Tanaquil	Tereza	Tita	Tzofia
Tancy	Terryl	Titania	Uda
Tandy	Tertia	Titian	Ulima
Tangerine	Tetty	Titiana	Ulla
Tangier	Texana	Tiuu	Ulrica
Tanis	Teyla	Tivona	Ultima
Tanith	Thaddea	Toccata	Uma
Tansy	Thaïs	Toinette	Umber
Tanwen	Thalassa	Topanga	Umbria
Taraja	Thames	Topaz	Umbrielle
Tarana	Thana	Tora	Umeko
Tarian	Thandie	Tordis	Undine
Tarot	Thanh	Toril	Unice
Tarragon	Theone	Torille	Unity
Tash	Theora	Tosca	Urania
Tasmine	Thérèse	Totty	Urban
Tate	Thessaly	Toula	Urbana
Tatjana	Thetis	Tova	Uriela
Taura	Thirza	Tove	Ursa
Tauria	Thisbe	Traveler	Uta
Tavi	Thomasa	Tribeca	Utah
Tavia	Thomasin	Trillian	Vala
Tavora	Thyme	Tristana	Valda
Tay	Tibbie	Trixie	Valeska
Taye	Tibby	Tu	Valetta

Vali	Vespera	Wendell	Yaiza
Valley	Vevina	West	Yale
Valo	Via	Whit	Yalena
Valora	Vianne	Whitman	Yamina
Vanda	Vica	Whizdom	Yana
Vanille	Vicenza	Wilfreda	Yara
Vanita	Victoire	Wilhelmiina	Yardley
Vanja	Vieira	Williamina	Yarrow
Vanna	Vienna	Windsor	Yeardley
Varana	Viera	Winola	Yeats
Varda	Vigdis	Winslet	Yehudit
Varinia	Vigee	Winslow	Yekaterina
Varsha	Viktorie	Winsome	Yelena
Varvara	Villette	Wisdom	Yevgeniya
Varya	Vincent	Wisteria	Ynez
Vasilia	Vincentia	Wren	Yoko
Vedette	Violante	Wylda	Yona
Vega	Vionnet	Wylie	Yonina
Vegas	Virgil	Wynn	Yori
Velouté	Virgilia	Wynonna	Yoshi
Vendela	Virtue	Wyoming	Ysabel
Venetia	Vittoria	Xabrina	Yseult
Venezia	Viveca	Xandra	Yudita
Ventura	Vivi	Xanthe	Yui
Verbena	Vivia	Xanthene	Yuki
Verdad	Vivica	Xanthippe	Yule
Verde	Viviette	Xantho	Yulia
Verdi	Vrai	Xaviera	Yvaine
Verina	Wade	Xen	Zabana
Verity	Walburga	Xenia	Zafira
Vermilion	Walda	Xenobia	Zagora
Vernon	Walker	Xia	Zahara
Veronika	Wallace	Xiamara	Zahava
Veronique	Wallis	Ximenia	Zahira
Véronique	Waverly	Xin	Zaina
Veruca	Wednesday	Xois	Zaira
Verve	Welcome	Yael	Zakia
Vesper	Wellesley	Yaffa	Zala

Zalika
Zaltana
Zambezi
Zamora
Zàn
Zaneta
Zaniah
Zanna
Zarela
Zarina
Zariza
Zarouhi
Zarya
Zathura
Zayna
Zaza
Zea
Zeborah
Zee
Zehava
Zeila
Zeke
Zelah
Zelena
Zelenia
Zelenka
Zelie
Zelina
Zelkova
Zemora
Zen
Zenaida
Zenda
Zephyr
Zephyrine
Zera
Zhanna
Zhen

Zia
Zilke
Zilla
Zinaida
Zinnia
Zippora
Zipporah
Ziva
Zivanka
Zixi
Ziza
Zizi
Zofia
Zohara
Zoia
Zoila
Zooey
Zorah
Zoraida
Zorina
Zosia
Zosma
Zoya
Zsa
Zsazsa
Zsófia
Zuelia
Zuleika
Zulma
Zuwena
Zuzanna
Zuzela
Zuzi
Zuzu

BOYS

Aakil	Acker	Aja	Alejo
Aalto	Actaeon	Ajamu	Aleph
Aart	Acton	Ajani	Alessio
Aaru	Adagio	Ajax	Alexei
Abacus	Adaiah	Akbar	Alexios
Aban	Adair	Akello	Alimayu
Abán	Adalius	Aki	Alistair
Abanito	Addar	Akim	Almonzo
Abanu	Adelio	Akiro	Alric
Abba	Adeon	Akiva	Altair
Abbas	Adhit	Aksel	Alun
Abdalla	Adil	Aladdin	Alvar
Abdallah	Adir	Alain	Álvaro
Abdu	Adiv	Alamo	Alwyn
Abeeku	Adolphe	Alani	Amadeo
Abelard	Adonijah	Alard	Amadeus
Aberdeen	Adriano	Alaric	Amadi
Abi	Aegis	Alarik	Amael
Abiah	Aeneas	Alasdair	Amahl
Abiel	Aesop	Alastair	Amato
Abijah	Agassi	Alban	Amaury
Abilene	Agni	Albany	Amazu
Abimael	Agu	Albee	Amedeo
Abir	Agung	Alben	Amedeus
Abraxas	Ahab	Albus	Amen
Absalom	Ahearne	Alcott	America
Abt	Ahman	Aldous	Amias
Abush	Aimilios	Aldrich	Amiel
Achille	Ainsley	Aleem	Amis
Achilles	Aio	Alef	Ammiras

Amory	Arkady	Auster	Balliol
Amphion	Arledge	Avdel	Ballou
Amsterdam	Arliss	Averil	Balsam
Amyas	Armistead	Averill	Balthasar
Amzi	Armstrong	Avi	Balthazar
Anastasios	Arnau	Aviv	Baltimore
Anchor	Aroon	Axl	Balton
Andor	Arpad	Ayu	Balzac
André	Arran	Aza	Bamboo
Andrés	Arrigo	Azaiah	Banan
Androcles	Arrio	Azariah	Bancroft
Aneurin	Arrow	Azarias	Bandit
Angaros	Arroyo	Aziel	Bangkok
Angelico	Artemas	Azizi	Banjo
Anse	Artemis	Azrael	Banner
Anselm	Aruna	Azriel	Banning
Anselmo	Arye	Azzam	Banyan
Antonius	Asahel	Azzedine	Baptiste
Aodh	Asaiah	Babson	Barabbas
Aoibheann	Ash	Bacchus	Barack
Apollinaire	Ashe	Bach	Barak
Apollos	Ashur	Bachelor	Baram
Aquilo	Asmund	Badar	Barbeau
Ara	Aspen	Baden	Barber
Araby	Aston	Bader	Barbossa
Aragon	Attila	Baer	Barclay
Aram	Atu	Baez	Bard
Aramis	Auberon	Baggio	Barden
Argento	Aubin	Bahram	Bardo
Argo	Auburn	Bain	Bardolf
Argus	Auden	Bainbridge	Bardrick
Argyle	Audio	Baird	Barker
Aries	Augusten	Baku	Barley
Aristedes	Augusto	Balbo	Barlow
Aristotle	Aurélien	Baldemar	Barn
Arjan	Aurelius	Balfour	Barnabas
Arkadi	Auric	Balin	Barnaby

Barnes	Bechet	Berilo	Bligh
Barnum	Beck	Berin	Blue
Barr	Becker	Berkeley	Bly
Barric	Bede	Bern	Boaz
Bartleby	Beech	Berold	Boden
Bartlett	Behan	Berquist	Bodi
Bartram	Beige	Berthold	Bogart
Baruch	Bela	Berwin	Bogdan
Bas	Belcher	Bevan	Bohan
Basie	Belden	Bevin	Bohdan
Baskara	Belisario	Bevis	Bolan
Bassett	Bellamy	Bezai	Bolivar
Bastian	Bello	Biaggio	Bolivia
Bastien	Bellow	Bickford	Bolton
Bates	Belvedere	Biff	Boman
Bauer	Benaiah	Bige	Bombay
Baxley	Benajah	Bimini	Bonanza
Bay	Benedetto	Bing	Bonaventure
Bayless	Benen	Bingham	Bond
Bayou	Benevolent	Bingo	Boniface
Bayu	Benicio	Birch	Bono
Baz	Benigno	Birkett	Booth
Baze	Benning	Birley	Borden
Bazel	Benno	Birney	Borromeo
Beacan	Benoit	Birtle	Bosco
Beach	Benoît	Bix	Bosley
Beacon	Benoni	Bjergen	Boswell
Beal	Benvenuto	Bjornson	Botan
Beale	Benvolio	Black	Botham
Beaman	Benyamin	Blackburn	Bourbon
Beamer	Bered	Blackwell	Bourne
Bear	Berenger	Blade	Bouvier
Bearchán	Beresford	Blakely	Bowie
Beathan	Berg	Blanco	Boyer
Beauchamp	Bergen	Blanford	Boyne
Beauregard	Berger	Blaque	Boynton
Becan	Beriah	Bleddyn	Bozrah

Bradan	Brewster	Burnet	Callahan
Bradbury	Brick	Burroughs	Callaway
Bradman	Bridge	Busby	Callister
Bradshaw	Brigham	Busch	Calloway
Braham	Briley	Butcher	Calm
Brahms	Brinley	Buxton	Calton
Brainard	Brinsley	Buzz	Calypso
Braison	Brio	Byatt	Canaan
Bram	Brishan	Byram	Canarsie
Bramwell	Bristol	Cab	Cándido
Bran	Britain	Cable	Canton
Branagan	Brockton	Cabot	Canute
Brand	Broder	Cadao	Canyon
Brandeis	Brodny	Caddock	Caolán
Brando	Brom	Cadell	Caradoc
Branigan	Bromley	Cadman	Carbry
Branley	Bron	Cadmus	Carden
Branton	Bronco	Cadoc	Carew
Braque	Brone	Cadogan	Carlin
Brason	Bronislaw	Caelan	Carlow
Bráulio	Bronx	Cager	Carlsen
Braun	Brooke	Cagney	Carmichael
Bravery	Brooklyn	Cailean	Carney
Bravo	Brosnan	Caio	Caro
Brawley	Brutus	Cairn	Carsten
Braxon	Bryn	Cairo	Caruso
Bray	Bubba	Caius	Carver
Braz	Buchanan	Calbert	Cashel
Brazier	Buckley	Calder	Caspar
Brazil	Buckminster	Caledon	Caspian
Breaker	Buff	Calen	Cassian
Breccan	Bunyan	Calendar	Cassiel
Breck	Burbank	Caliban	Castor
Breckin	Burford	California	Cathan
Brenner	Burgundy	Calix	Catullus
Bretton	Burma	Calixto	Cavan
Brevin	Burne	Callaghan	Cavanaugh

Cayman	Christo	Conaire	Crispin
Cayo	Christos	Conal	Crispus
Cedar	Churchill	Conall	Cristóbal
Celadon	Cian	Conan	Croix
Celio	Cianán	Concord	Cronan
Cellini	Ciar	Congo	Cronus
Cello	Ciaran	Conlan	Cross
Cerulean	Ciarán	Connelly	Crow
César	Cielo	Connery	Cuarto
Chalil	Cillian	Connolly	Cuba
Chan	Cinna	Conran	Culley
Chancellor	Cipriano	Conroy	Cullinan
Chaney	Ciro	Constant	Culver
Chang	Cisco	Constantin	Cupid
Chaniel	Claes	Coolio	Curran
Chapin	Clancy	Corby	Currier
Chaplin	Cleanth	Corcoran	Curry
Charaka	Cleary	Cord	Cuthbert
Charleston	Cleavon	Cordovan	Cutler
Charlot	Clete	Corentin	Cy
Chasen	Clooney	Corin	Cyan
Chasin	Cloud	Cork	Cymbeline
Chaucer	Clove	Cormac	Cyprian
Chavez	Cluny	Coro	Cyprus
Chaviv	Coal	Corrado	Cyrano
Chazaiah	Cobalt	Cort	Cyrille
Chazon	Coleridge	Cosimo	Daan
Ché	Coll	Cotton	Dacey
Cheever	Colm	Cougar	Dacian
Chelsea	Colman	Count	Daedalus
Chen	Colombe	Cove	Dafydd
Cheney	Colorado	Coz	Dag
Chevy	Coltrane	Crane	Dagwood
Chico	Colum	Cranston	Dahy
Chili	Columba	Craven	Dai
Chirico	Columbo	Creighton	Daire
Christmas	Como	Crichton	Daithi

Daley	Daxter	Dezi	Donnelly
Dalfon	Day	Dhani	Donough
Dalmazio	Deccan	Diarmaid	Dooley
Daly	December	Diaz	Doran
Dalziel	Decimus	Dice	Doron
Damario	Decker	Dickinson	Dorset
Damaso	Declare	Dickson	Dougal
Damek	Deepak	Didier	Dougray
Danar	Dei	Diesel	Dov
Dancer	Delaney	Dieter	Dove
Danger	Delgado	Dietrich	Dover
Dani	Delias	Digby	Dovev
Danilo	Delmore	Diji	Draco
Danner	Delroy	Dilwyn	Draper
Dano	Democracy	Dinand	Dream
Danton	Demos	Dingo	Drennon
Danube	Denali	Dinsmore	Dresden
Danya	Denham	Diogenes	Drover
Daoud	Denim	Dionysius	Drum
Daphnis	Deniz	Diplomacy	Drummer
Dara	Dennison	Discovery	Drummond
Darko	Deodar	Diversity	Dryden
Darragh	Derby	Dix	Drystan
Darrow	Dermot	Django	Duald
Darshan	Derry	Djimon	Dublin
Dart	Descartes	Dmitri	Duccio
D'artagnan	Deshan	Doane	Dugan
Darton	Desiderio	Dobbin	Dulé
Dasan	Deuce	Dodge	Dumas
Dash	Deveraux	Dodson	Dunbar
Dashiell	Devere	Doherty	Dundee
Dathan	Devlin	Dolan	Dune
Daumier	Devo	Domino	Dunham
Davenport	Devraj	Donahue	Dunn
Davidson	Dewi	Donar	Dunstan
Davies	Dex	Donatello	Duran
Daxon	Dez	Donnan	Durango

Durant	Elazer	Erskine	Faldo
Durham	Eleazar	Eryx	Falkner
Durie	Eleazer	Esai	Fallon
Duryea	Eleven	Esmond	Falmouth
Dushan	Elgar	Espen	Fane
Duvall	Elia	Etan	Fargo
Dweezil	Eliab	Etienne	Farley
Dyson	Eliakim	Étienne	Farmer
Eachann	Eliam	Ettore	Faro
Eagle	Elián	Euan	Farouk
Eames	Eliaz	Euston	Farquahar
Eamon	Elio	Evardo	Farquhar
Éamon	Eliphalet	Ever	Farrar
Earvin	Ellington	Everard	Faulkner
Eastman	Elm	Everest	Faust
Eaton	Eloi	Everly	Favorite
Eban	Elul	Evian	Favre
Eberhard	Elvio	Ewan	Faxon
Ebo	Embry	Experience	Fayette
Edan	Emeril	Explorer	Feeny
Edel	Emilien	Ezio	Feivel
Edi	Emlyn	Fabiano	Fennel
Edmundo	Emo	Fabio	Fenno
Edric	Emrys	Fable	Ferenc
Eelia	Endicott	Fabrice	Fergall
Eero	Endymion	Fabrizio	Fergus
Eetu	Engelbert	Fabron	Ferguson
Efron	Eno	Fachnan	Fermin
Egan	Eoghan	Factor	Field
Egon	Eoin	Fagin	Fielder
Egypt	Eóin	Fahd	Fiero
Eilam	Eónan	Fairbairn	Fife
Eilon	Ephai	Fairbanks	Fifer
Eitan	Erickson	Fairchild	Figueroa
Eja	Ericson	Fairfax	Filbert
Eladio	Erikson	Faisal	Filip
Elan	Eros	Falcon	Filmore

Finbar	Fox	Galo	Germain
Finch	Fran	Galt	Geronimo
Finesse	Franchot	Galton	Gershom
Fingal	François	Galvin	Gershwin
Finian	Frankito	Galway	Gervaise
Finlay	Fraser	Gamal	Giacomo
Finnian	Free	Gandolf	Gian
Finnigan	Freedom	Gandy	Gide
Fionn	Frey	Ganesh	Giffard
Fiorello	Friedrich	Gannet	Gig
Fiorenzo	Frisco	Garcia	Gilby
Fire	Fritzi	Gardener	Gilead
Fisk	Frodi	Gareth	Gili
Fitz	Frodo	Garian	Gillespie
Fitzroy	Frost	Garren	Giorgio
Fitzwilliam	Fuentes	Garson	Giotto
Flame	Fuji	Garvan	Giuliano
Flanagan	Fulbright	Garvey	Giulio
Flann	Future	Gaspar	Glade
Flannery	Fynn	Gatsby	Glasgow
Flash	Fyodor	Gauguin	Glyn
Flavian	Gabi	Gauthier	Gogol
Flavius	Gabin	Gautier	Goku
Fleetwood	Gable	Gavi	Goliath
Florent	Gabo	Gavriel	Gomer
Florin	Gábor	Gavriil	Göran
Fogarty	Gadiel	Gawain	Gore
Foley	Gaetan	Gedaliah	Goren
Folke	Gahan	Gehrig	Gorky
Fonso	Gahiji	Gehry	Gower
Forbes	Gaius	Gemini	Gram
Forever	Gal	Genesis	Gramercy
Forster	Galil	Genet	Granger
Fort	Galileo	Gentry	Granite
Fortitude	Gallagher	Georgi	Graziano
Fortney	Gallio	Geraint	Greco
Fortune	Galloway	Gerik	Greeley

Gregor	Hali	Havana	Hiawatha
Grey	Halian	Havard	Hidalgo
Griffey	Halifax	Havelock	Hideki
Guillaume	Halle	Hawaii	Hieronymous
Guillem	Halloran	Hawes	Hieronymus
Guitar	Halston	Hawk	Hikaru
Gull	Hamal	Hawthorne	Hilaire
Gulliver	Hamill	Haydn	Hillel
Günter	Hamish	Hazael	Hippolyte
Gunther	Hamlet	Hazaiah	Hiro
Guri	Hamlin	Hazard	Hiroto
Guryon	Hammett	Haze	History
Gwilym	Hammond	Hazelton	Hitch
Gwylym	Hamzah	Heathcliff	Hob
Gwyn	Hanan	Heddwyn	Hobbes
Gyan	Hancock	Hedeon	Hodgson
Gyuri	Hanif	Heinrich	Hogan
Haakon	Hanish	Heinz	Holt
Habakkuk	Hannibal	Heladio	Honoré
Habib	Hanno	Helgi	Hooker
Hackett	Hanoch	Helio	Hooper
Haco	Harbin	Heller	Hopper
Hadar	Harbor	Helmut	Horizon
Hadden	Hari	Helsinki	Horst
Hadrian	Harlem	Hemingway	Horus
Hadriel	Harmony	Hendrik	Houghton
Hagan	Haroun	Hendrix	Howe
Hagrid	Harp	Henley	Howel
Haig	Harpo	Hercules	Hubbell
Haim	Harrington	Hermes	Huck
Haines	Harte	Hernando	Huckleberry
Haji	Hartigan	Hero	Huffington
Hakan	Hartman	Heron	Hulbert
Halcyon	Hartwig	Herrick	Humbert
Haldan	Haruki	Hervé	Hume
Haldor	Harvard	Hesperos	Huntington
Haley	Haskel	Hewett	Huntley

Huon	Increase	Jannick	Jevin
Huracan	Indiana	Jannik	Jex
Hurst	Indio	Janos	Jinjur
Hussein	Ingmar	János	Jiro
Hutchings	Inigo	Janson	Joab
Huxley	Iniko	Jantzen	Joachim
Hyatt	Innes	January	Joah
Hyde	Innocent	Janus	Jock
Iago	Ioan	Japheth	Johannes
Iain	Iolo	Japhy	Jolyon
Iakona	Ion	Jareb	Jonty
Ianto	Isandro	Jarek	Joop
Ianu	Ishaq	Jareth	Joost
Ib	Issey	Jari	Joplin
Ibo	Italo	Jarlath	Jorah
Ibsen	Ivanhoe	Jarman	Jor-El
Icarus	Ivar	Jas	Jorgen
Ichabod	Ives	Jati	José
Ichiro	Ivo	Javan	Joss
Ickitt	Izak	Javelin	Jotham
Idan	Izar	Jaz	Jothan
Idi	Izidor	Jazz	Jove
Ido	Izzy	Jebediah	Jubal
Ieuan	Jabin	Jedaiah	Jud
Ifor	Jac	Jehu	Judas
Igashu	Jachin	Jem	Jun
Iggy	Jacinto	Jenkin	Juneau
Igor	Jaco	Jeppe	Junot
Iku	Jacobo	Jericho	Jupiter
Ilan	Jago	Jermajesty	Kaddish
Ilara	Jaguar	Jerrick	Kadir
Ilari	Jahan	Jersey	Kaelan
Ilario	Jaka	Jerzy	Kafka
Ilie	Jalmari	Jestin	Kaiis
Ilya	Jamieson	Jesús	Kaj
Imari	Janek	Jet	Kálmán
Imre	Janne	Jeter	Kamal

Kamil	Khalíl	Lakota	Lexus
Kaniel	Kiah	Lancaster	Liberato
Kannon	Kier	Lancelot	Liev
Kano	Kiernan	Land	Light
Karel	Kiran	Lander	Lintang
Kari	Kito	Lando	Lito
Karmi	Kitt	Laney	Litton
Karsten	Kitto	Lanford	Livingston
Kasper	Klaus	Langdon	Llew
Kato	Klee	Langley	Lleyton
Kavan	Klemens	Langston	Loch
Kavanaugh	Knight	Lanier	Lochlainn
Kea	Knut	Laramie	Locke
Keahi	Kofi	Lardner	Lodge
Kean	Kojo	Laredo	Loeb
Keane	Kolya	Laszlo	Loew
Keats	Konrad	Latham	Loewy
Keefe	Kool	Latif	Loic
Keeley	Korben	Laughlin	Loman
Keen	Koren	Laurent	Lonan
Kees	Kort	Lauro	Londyn
Keir	Kostya	Laver	Longfellow
Keiran	Krishna	Lazarus	Lorcan
Kellam	Kristof	Lazer	Lord
Kelso	Kumar	Leaf	Lothar
Kemuel	Kwan	Leandre	Loudon
Kenelm	Kyd	Leary	Lowe
Kenn	Kynaston	Lebron	Lucan
Kennelly	Kyoto	Lech	Lucretius
Kensington	Laban	Leib	Ludlow
Kenzie	Lachlan	Leith	Ludovic
Kenzo	Lacrosse	Lennan	Lundy
Kerouac	Ladd	Leno	Lynch
Kerr	Lael	Leone	Lynx
Kesey	Lafcadio	Leonid	Lyon
Kester	Laird	Lev	Lysander
Keyne	Lake	Leviticus	Macaulay

Macdonald	Manolo	Melchior	Monico
Macgregor	Mansur	Melker	Montague
Machi	Manu	Melky	Montego
Maclean	Manus	Melor	Montez
Macon	Manzie	Menashe	Moore
Madigan	Manzo	Mendel	Morandi
Madoc	Manzu	Menzies	Mordecai
Mael	Maoz	Merce	Mori
Magee	Marceau	Mercury	Morley
Maggio	March	Meshach	Moroccan
Magic	Marino	Meteor	Morocco
Magnus	Marlow	Mica	Morpheus
Maguire	Marlowe	Micaiah	Morrie
Mahmoud	Marmaduke	Micajah	Morrisey
Mahomet	Mars	Micha	Morrison
Maillol	Marsden	Michaiah	Morrissey
Majesty	Marston	Micheál	Moss
Majid	Maso	Michelangelo	Mowgli
Makari	Massai	Mick	Mozart
Makis	Massey	Midnight	Muir
Malachy	Massimo	Mies	Mulligan
Málik	Mathis	Mikko	Mungo
Malin	Matisse	Miklós	Munro
Maliq	Mattias	Milos	Mykelti
Malloy	Maxen	Ming	Naaman
Malo	Maxence	Mingus	Nabil
Malone	Maxfield	Mirin	Nacho
Maloney	Maxime	Miró	Nachum
Malus	Mayer	Mirren	Nacio
Mandela	Mccanna	Mischa	Nadim
Mandla	Mccoy	Misha	Nadir
Mando	Mcdermott	Moby	Naeem
Manfred	Mcenroe	Moisés	Nagel
Manju	Mcewan	Moishe	Nahir
Mannix	Mead	Mojave	Nahma
Manny	Mees	Molloy	Naim
Mano	Meir	Mongo	Nairn

Nairobi	Nazareth	Nicolai	November
Naji	Nazih	Nicolo	Noyce
Najib	Neander	Nicolò	Numair
Nakos	Nebo	Nicomedes	Nuncio
Nakotah	Nectarios	Niels	Nuri
Naldo	Neel	Night	Nuriel
Nalin	Negasi	Nike	Nuru
Namaka	Nehru	Nikita	Nye
Namid	Nelius	Nikos	Oak
Namir	Nelly	Nikostratos	Oakes
Nando	Nelo	Nila	Oan
Nansen	Nemesio	Nilo	Obadiah
Naor	Nemo	Nilsson	Obadias
Naphtali	Nen	Nima	Obama
Napier	Neo	Nimrod	Oberon
Naquan	Neptune	Nin	Obi
Narain	Nereus	Ninian	O'brian
Narcissus	Nero	Nino	Obrien
Nardo	Neruda	Niño	O'brien
Naren	Nesbit	Nir	O'callahan
Narve	Nevada	Niran	O'casey
Nashua	Neville	Nishan	Ocean
Nasim	Newbold	Nissan	Oceanus
Nasser	Newbury	Niven	O'connor
Natal	Newland	Njord	Odhran
Nate	Newlin	Noam	Odilio
Naum	Newport	Noaz	Odion
Navarone	Nguyen	Nohea	Odissan
Navarro	Niall	Nollie	Ödön
Naveed	Nicabar	Noon	O'donnell
Navigator	Nicandro	Norfolk	O'donovan
Navin	Nicasio	Nori	Odysseus
Naviyd	Nicholson	Northcliff	Oedipus
Navy	Nickleby	Northrop	O'fallon
Nayland	Nickolai	Norville	O'grady
Naylor	Nicodemus	Norvin	Ogun
Nazaire	Nicol	Nouvel	Ohan

Ohara	Oskar	Paladio	Patrin
O'hara	Oslo	Palani	Patterson
Oisin	Osman	Palash	Patton
Oisín	Osmond	Palben	Patxi
Ojai	Osric	Palermo	Paulin
O'keefe	Ossian	Paley	Pavel
Okello	Ossin	Palin	Pavlo
Oleg	O'sullivan	Palomo	Pawnee
Olimpio	Oswin	Palti	Pax
Olivier	Othello	Pan	Payne
Olsen	Ottavio	Panas	Paz
Olympos	Oxford	Pancho	Pazel
Omega	Oz	Panos	Peabody
Omri	Ozias	Panya	Peace
O'neal	Ozni	Paolo	Peadair
Onslow	Ozuru	Paquito	Peak
Ontario	Ozzy	Paramesh	Peale
Onyx	Paavo	Parc	Pearce
O'reilly	Pace	Parish	Peder
Orel	Paciano	Parkin	Peel
Orestes	Pacific	Parnell	Peerless
Orev	Packard	Parr	Pei
Orfeo	Paco	Parren	Pelagios
Ori	Pacome	Parry	Pelé
Oriol	Paddy	Parson	Pelham
Ornette	Paden	Parthalán	Pelí
Orno	Padget	Parthenios	Pell
Oro	P'adraic	Parton	Pelle
Orpheus	Padraig	Parvaiz	Pellegrino
Orsino	Pádraig	Pascoe	Pelli
Ortega	Pagan	Pasha	Pello
Osbert	Pagiel	Pashenka	Pembroke
Osgood	Paine	Pasqual	Pendleton
O'shea	Painter	Pastor	Penley
Osheen	Paisley	Paterson	Penn
Osias	Palace	Patrice	Penrod
Osiris	Paladin	Patricio	Penrose

Pepa	Phipps	Pollock	Qadar
Pepe	Phoebus	Pollux	Qadim
Pepin	Phyllon	Polo	Qadir
Pepper	Piano	Pom	Qamar
Per	Picabia	Pomeroy	Qasim
Perdido	Picard	Pompey	Quade
Peregrine	Picasso	Ponce	Quaid
Perez	Pickford	Ponti	Quain
Perfecto	Pierluigi	Porat	Quanah
Pericles	Piero	Poriel	Quantavius
Perico	Piers	Porthos	Quarry
Perkin	Piet	Portland	Quartz
Perseus	Pietro	Poseidon	Quay
Persia	Pike	Potter	Quebec
Perth	Pili	Power	Quennel
Peru	Pilot	Powers	Quest
Pervis	Pinchas	Powhatan	Quico
Pesah	Pine	Pradeep	Quigley
Peterson	Pino	Prairie	Quill
Peteul	Pio	Praxis	Quillan
Petiri	Pip	Prescott	Quillen
Petrini	Piper	Prewitt	Quiller
Peverell	Pippin	Priam	Quilliam
Pharaoh	Piran	Priest	Quillon
Phelan	Pitney	Primo	Quimby
Phelix	Pitt	Proctor	Quince
Phelps	Placido	Prosperity	Quinlan
Philadelphia	Plato	Prospero	Quinney
Philander	Platt	Proust	Quintas
Philbert	Plaxico	Provo	Quintero
Philemon	Plenty	Prys	Quinto
Philippe	Pluto	Ptolemy	Quintus
Philomon	Po	Puck	Quirin
Philosophy	Poe	Purvis	Quirinal
Phinean	Pol	Putnam	Quirino
Phineas	Poldi	Pyotr	Quirt
Phinnaeus	Pollard	Pyramid	Quito

Quixley

Quixote

Quon

Ra

Raanan

Rabi

Racer

Racham

Rad

Radburn

Radcliff

Radley

Raeburn

Rafaele

Rafferty

Rafi

Rafiq

Ragnar

Rahim

Rain

Rainer

Raines

Rainier

Rajah

Rajiv

Ralphie

Ralston

Ram

Rambo

Ramón

Ramone

Ramsay

Ramses

Rancher

Ranger

Rani

Ranjit

Ranulph

Rashid

Rasmus

Raúl

Ravi

Rawlins

Rawson

Raynor

Read

Reading

Rebel

Rebop

Redford

Reef

Reeve

Rego

Rem

Rembrandt

Remi

Remo

Remus

Rémy

Ren

Renato

Renaud

René

Rennon

Renny

Renon

Renzo

Reo

Reynard

Rhodes

Rhodri

Riah

Richart

Rider

Ridley

Rigby

Ring

Ringo

Rio

Riordan

Rip

Ripley

Ritter

Riyad

Roald

Roan

Roark

Robbe

Robertson

Robinson

Roc

Rochester

Rocket

Rocko

Rockwell

Rodion

Rodman

Rodriguez

Rogan

Rogue

Rohmer

Rojo

Romanus

Romany

Romelo

Romer

Romney

Romulus

Romy

Rondel

Roni

Ronson

Roone

Rooney

Roper

Roreto

Rosh

Roth

Rousseau

Roux

Rowley

Roxbury

Royden

Royston

Ruby

Rudyard

Rue

Rugby

Rule

Rumo

Rune

Runyon

Rusk

Ruskin

Rye

Saad

Saar

Sabik

Sabin

Sabino

Sabir

Sabo

Sacha

Sacheverell

Sadaka

Sadik

Sahaj

Sahil

Sahir

Sa'id

Sailor

Sajan

Saladin

Salah

Salem

Salim

Salinger

Salix

Salman

Salmon

Salton

Salvator

Samal

Samar

Sami

Samo

Sancho

Sander

Sanderson

Sandor

Sandros

Sanjay

Sanjaya

Sanjiro

Sansone

Sarad

Sargent

Sarkis

Saroyan

Sarto

Sascha

Sasha

Satchel

Satriya

Saturn

Savva

Sax

Saxon

Sayer

Science

Scipio

Scorpio

Scout

Scully

Seagull

Seal

Sealey

Seanán

Seaton

Seb

Seeger

Segundo

Seiji

Selby

Selig

Selwyn

Sem

Senegal

Sennett

Septimus

Sequoyah

Seraphim

Seren

Sereno

Serge

Sergeant

Sergei

Seumas

Sevan

Seven

Severin

Severus

Sextus

Shabaan

Shai

Shakespeare

Shale

Shalom

Shamir

Shamus

Shanahan

Shandar

Shandy

Shango

Shaqir

Shaviv

Shaw

Shawnel

Sheehan

Sheffield

Shem

Sherlock

Shia

Shiloh

Shimon

Shiron

Shlomo

Shmuel

Sholto

Siâm

Siegfried

Sierra

Silvain

Silvano

Simba

Simcha

Simm

Sinbad

Sinclair

Sindri

Sinjon

Sion

Siôn

Siôr

Siraj

Sirius

Siro

Sisqó

Sisyphus

Sixtus

Skeet

Skipper

Sky

Skye

Slate

Slater

Sloane

Sly

Socrates

Soho

Sören

Sorley

Sorrel

Sorrell

Sosthenes

Soutine

Spalding

Speck

Spike

Spiro

Springer

Spruce

Squall

Stamatios

Stamos

Stancio

Stanislav	Tabor	Tay	Thoreau
Stavros	Taddeo	Taye	Thorne
Stedman	Taden	Tayson	Thorpe
Steel	Tadeo	Teague	Thurber
Stefano	Tadhg	Teal	Thurgood
Stellan	Taffy	Teel	Thurstan
Stellen	Taggart	Teilo	Tiberius
Sten	Tahmel	Temani	Tibor
Stephanos	Tahoe	Temple	Tide
Stephanus	Taiden	Templeton	Tiernan
Steveland	Tait	Tempo	Tierney
Stian	Takeo	Tennessee	Tiger
Stig	Talbot	Tennyson	Timaeus
Stijn	Talcott	Terach	Timber
Stirling	Talib	Terre	Timo
Story	Taliesin	Tertius	Timon
Street	Talman	Teton	Tino
Striker	Tam	Tew	Tip
Strom	Tamarack	Texas	Tiras
Struan	Tamerlane	Thackeray	Tobiah
Suede	Tamir	Thane	Tolliver
Sufjan	Tamlane	Thanh	Tomás
Suhul	Tancred	Thanos	Tomasso
Sulaiman	Tancredo	Thatcher	Tomasz
Sulien	Tane	Thayer	Tommaso
Sully	Tangier	Thelonious	Tonio
Sultan	Tango	Thelonius	Topher
Sunny	Tanguy	Theobald	Tor
Sutcliff	Taos	Theodoric	Torin
Sutton	Tarak	Theon	Torquil
Sven	Tarian	Theophilos	Toulouse
Swain	Tarot	Theophilus	Toussaint
Sweden	Tarquin	Theseus	Tovi
Sweeney	Tarzan	Thibault	Tower
Swithun	Tasso	Thierry	Track
Syrus	Tavis	Thijs	Trail
Tabari	Tavish	Thom	Traveler

Traylor	Uri	Venturi	Vrai
Treat	Urien	Venturo	Vulcan
Tremont	Urso	Venya	Wagner
Trenner	Usher	Verdi	Wainwright
Trig	Ushi	Vered	Walden
Trip	Utah	Vermont	Wales
Tristram	Uz	Vernados	Warrick
Trout	Uzi	Vero	Welby
Tru	Uziah	Verrill	Wenczeslaw
Trust	Uzziah	Vesper	Werther
Truth	Vachel	Vesuvio	Westbrook
Tucson	Václav	Vicus	Westcott
Tudor	Vadim	Vidar	Wharton
Tulio	Vail	Vidor	Whistler
Tully	Valdemar	Viggo	Whitford
Turtle	Valerian	Vijay	Whittaker
Twain	Valerio	Vikram	Wild
Tynan	Vallis	Vilhelm	Wilder
Typhoon	Valo	Viliam	Wilkes
Udell	Valor	Viljo	Willem
Ugo	Valter	Villard	Willoughby
Uilleam	Vandal	Villiers	Wills
Uilliam	Vandyke	Vin	Wim
Ulan	Vane	Vine	Windsor
Ulf	Vanya	Ving	Winslow
Ulick	Varan	Vinny	Winter
Ull	Vardon	Vireo	Wizard
Ulric	Vasant	Viridian	Wolcott
Ultan	Vasco	Vischer	Wolf
Umar	Vasili	Vishnu	Wolfgang
Umber	Vaughan	Vittorio	Wolverine
Umberto	Ved	Vitus	Worthy
Unai	Veer	Vivaldo	Wray
Unika	Vega	Vlad	Wyclef
Unique	Venedictos	Vladimir	Wylei
Upton	Venezio	Vladislav	Wyn
Upwood	Venn	Volante	Wyndham

Wynton	Yukio	Zayd	Zoilo
Wystan	Yul	Zbigniew	Zola
Xan	Yule	Zebedee	Zoltan
Xanthos	Yuma	Zebediah	Zooey
Xanthus	Yuri	Zebulun	Zophar
Xen	Yves	Zedekiah	Zorion
Xenophon	Zabe	Zeév	Zubin
Xenos	Zac	Zeki	Zuri
Xerxes	Zaccheus	Zelig	Zvi
Ximenes	Zach	Zell	Zyler
Xylon	Zachalie	Zelmo	
Yada	Zacharias	Zen	
Yakim	Zade	Zenobios	
Yakov	Zaden	Zeo	
Yale	Zadock	Zephaniah	
Yanai	Zadornin	Zephyr	
Yancey	Zafar	Zephyrin	
Yanis	Zahavi	Zeppelin	
Yann	Zahir	Zerah	
Yannick	Zahn	Zero	
Yannis	Zailey	Zerrick	
Yarden	Zair	Zeru	
Yardley	Zak	Zesiro	
Yaron	Zaki	Zeus	
Yarrow	Zakk	Zevadiah	
Yasha	Zako	Zevi	
Yasir	Zale	Zevon	
Yeats	Zalmai	Zhivago	
Yehudah	Zalman	Zia	
Yevgeny	Zamiel	Ziggy	
Yisrael	Zamir	Zikomo	
Yitzhak	Zan	Zimran	
Yonah	Zandy	Zinc	
Yorick	Zared	Zinedine	
Yosemite	Zarney	Ziv	
Yoshi	Zarren	Ziven	
Yu	Zavid	Zohar	